If God is So Good, Why Do I Always Seem to be Broke?

Paul Plagerson

PUBLISHING

Endorsements

We have had the privilege of walking with Paul (and his wonderful wife, Anne) for a number of years and are so grateful for them. Here is a couple who are not only passionate for Jesus, but who have translated that passion into wisdom, integrity and kindness in their every day life. This book is full of insights from Scripture married with incredibly practical advice for stewarding your finances. It is thoughtful, inspiring and very helpful. What a privilege to learn from Paul - a man who lives what he preaches and has the generosity to share what he has learnt.

Julian and Katia Adams
Leaders of The Table, Boston
Directors of Frequentsee

Short, life changing, and profound. What more could you want? Biblical, pastoral and practical too. Paul Plagerson has written an important book that is a must-read for anyone who has tried to navigate well intentioned but contradictory church teaching on money.

Chris Bullivant
Writer and Political Commentator

This Money Book is provocative, challenging and full of wisdom. Paul wants us to foster an expectation of prosperity ... so that we can also be generous. Starting with the Bible, interesting illustrations and stories, it then gets very practical. This book will make you think, pray and then get out your calculator! It has been great sitting down with Paul for this very timely financial review!

Rob Davey
Senior Pastor, Jubilee Church, Solihull

Paul is a much-loved friend and wise counsellor going back many years. His wisdom and faithful prayers have helped steer Caroline and I both financially but also in many other ways. I am so delighted for you to get to read this book, which is an incredible resource for the church today. Few books deal so directly with money and even fewer give understanding to the spiritual, emotional and mental underpinnings of our finances.

Paul does both things brilliantly in this book and I know that anyone who follows through with the practical and spiritual wisdom found here will set themselves up on a solid financial foundation. Read it, apply it and be transformed by it!

Simon Holley

Senior Leader, King's Arms Church and Catalyst Team Leader

Paul's wise advice comes from decades of experience both as a professional in financial services and as a follower of Jesus. He speaks with honesty and sincerity providing a great mixture of biblical wisdom and practical wisdom. His teaching is worth listening to & applying to your life.

David Stroud

Senior Pastor, Christ Church London, co-founder, Everything Conference

Jesus taught on finance and wealth more than almost any other subject, because he understood that money is a mirror that shows us something about God and something about ourselves. Money is a canvas on which God reveals Himself and us. Paul Plagerson has written the book on money I wish I had been able to read 20 years ago because he tackles this vital subject in such an honest, faith-filled, wise and ultimately biblical way. In reading it you will be equipped to live free from poverty thinking but also be content in every circumstance. This is a brilliant book and in reading it you will be challenged but also changed.

Phil Wilthew

Author of *Developing Prophetic Culture* and *Multiplying Disciples*

I have known Paul for over 30 years and seen the way he has lived life both in family and business. I have tasted fruit in these two areas both by knowing his family and working within his business. There isn't much of a tougher testing ground for life, not just listening to a person's words but watching the 'seedbed' of their actions and the fruit it produces. Such actions have been shaped by skilful principles that Paul and Anne have learned from the most skilful adviser of them all …. and then they have put them into practice. Now that is wisdom!

Chris Vincent

Financial Adviser

British Library Cataloguing in Publication Data
A catalogue record for this book is available from the British Library.
ISBN 978-1-912863-52-5

Cover design by Angela Selfe
Art direction by Sarah Grace
Printed in the UK

Dedication

For my children.
This is what I hoped I taught you about money and the goodness of
God as you grew up.
Here it is for you to teach to your children.

Contents

Contents

Introduction

Have you ever wondered why you seem to be struggling financially, and why whatever money you make never seems to be enough? Then this book is for you. Most advice about money seems to be delivered either by people who have made their first million before they were out of school and want to show you that you can do it too, or by those who micromanage their cash and adjust their lifestyles, to show that by getting the best deals you can live on less than you ever thought possible.

This book is an attempt to look at wealth from a balanced scriptural perspective. My purpose is to help you identify and remove some blockages on the road to prosperity. There is no poverty in heaven, and we are instructed to pray 'on earth as it is in heaven'. So we should not only be praying that prayer but also experiencing the results. God has provided a wonderful creation for his people to care for and enjoy. He has placed us in charge of a beautiful planet. Should we not be enjoying its fruits? I will attempt to demonstrate from scripture that an abundant life is the birthright of those who seek to follow Jesus. However, that abundant life does not happen automatically; it has to be appropriated by faith, prayer and wise action.

Some years ago I found myself in a difficult situation. I had recently been appointed to church eldership but at the same time found myself in debt with arrears on my mortgage, almost to the point of repossession of my house by the bank. Imagine my conflicting emotions. I felt blessed and respected in the congregation and yet wrestled with sometimes overwhelming feelings of guilt and shame, as well as the fear that someone would discover my situation and I would be exposed as a fraud. I had a wife and three young children dependent on me as provider and I could not believe I had allowed this to happen. What made things worse was that I was a professional financial adviser, helping others manage their money!

God always responds to desperate prayer and provides a way through difficult situations, even if it is not always the route we are hoping for. I was blessed with a friend who was a Christian bank manager to whom I finally confessed my predicament. He was able to allow me to add the arrears to my mortgage to resolve my debt and gradually catch up with my payments.

How had I arrived in this situation? I was working for a Christian company that ran into difficulties and had to reduce my salary, leaving me unable to pay all my bills. I learned many lessons from that time, not least the fact that just because you were a Christian did not necessarily protect you from economic reality and an employer's incompetence. Resolving that I would never allow that issue to arise again, I set out to understand better the workings of money management, and why some people were blessed financially yet others seemed always to be struggling to survive.

My background

Over many years as a financial adviser, I have taught and counselled people about their personal finances and discovered that, for the great majority, their attitude towards money was shaped by their upbringing and the attitudes prevalent at home when they were growing up. The first step to financial understanding is recognising our existing attitudes towards money and the source of those attitudes. Whether you handle your money just like your parents or you have reacted against how they managed their money, it is those early years that shape us.

As I looked at my own background, I could start to see how my father's attitudes had shaped me. I am from a middle-class Jewish family in the North of England. My father had inherited a small business from his father, who had arrived in this country from Lithuania as an asylum seeker, and had started a wholesale watch and clock company. My father worked hard and with his brothers built a reasonable business.

After the Second World War, however, people's expectations began to change. Having endured a long period of austerity, customers wanted choice and fashion, not just the cheapest way of telling the time, and the family business struggled to adapt to changing consumer demands. My father formed the underlying belief that making a living is difficult. His response to others who were prospering in the same line of business was suspicion that they must be doing something underhand or illegal.

My mother's family were altogether more entrepreneurial. Her father had built up a successful clothing manufacturing company and was doing well. I can remember the thrill as a small boy of sitting in my grandfather's shiny new Daimler. My mother grew up with a much more relaxed attitude towards money; she was generous and charitable. Perhaps you can imagine some of our family conflicts regarding finance. My father watched the pennies and my mother gave away the pounds! I grew up, therefore, believing that making a living was difficult, yet enjoying spending at the same time. Perhaps that is why I found myself in that difficult situation with my mortgage. Having grown up in a relatively comfortably off middle-class family, I felt a complete failure because of my financial struggles. I could not quite grasp why I wasn't rich.

When I became a believer in Jesus, however, I found that the church of which I had become a member not only seemed to regard poverty as acceptable but almost seemed to revel in it as a sign of holiness. This appeared to be a contradiction that I found difficult to understand. This new covenant seemed to have heavenly and spiritual blessings, it had Jesus and the Holy Spirit, but apparently no material benefits. The old covenant had material blessings for following the Law - but a distant God. If the new covenant was better than the old, why should a believer be poorer under the new? Shouldn't the blessings of the new be in *addition* to the blessings of the old? It did not appear to make sense.

Nobody I had met in my years as a financial adviser admitted to growing up with the specific ambition to be poor. I had met plenty of people who were poor, many of whom could not understand why, but no one who said that being poor was one of their life's ambitions. There are people who see being poor as a sign of holiness, others who believe that being poor is just one of those quirks of fate over which we have no control. Some people think they are just not smart enough to be rich, others feel their poverty is a punishment for sin or lack of financial self-control. Poverty is relative, and many in the western world who consider themselves poor would be deemed wealthy in many parts of the developing world. My particular concern is with Christians in the west who either believe that poverty is synonymous with holiness or feel that they have no control over or understanding of money. They believe that the flow of their finances just happens to them, like the weather, not because of their beliefs or actions.

Sometimes poverty is a result of birth and environment. Many countries in Africa, Asia and South America are really poor. But they don't have to be. There are enough resources in the world to go around. The basic problem is one of distribution rather than overall shortage. According to a recent study published in the journal

Nature Sustainability,[2] the world already grows enough food for 10 billion people. It does seem that wherever there are poor people there are rich ones as well. In all these developing countries, one will find those who are wealthy, usually closely related to the ruling political leadership, often with very large foreign bank accounts and properties overseas.

The reasons for world hunger are beyond the scope of this book. Rather, I wish to show that generous, prosperous Christians could be a large part of the answer. Most of us, when asked if we would rather be rich or poor, would think that a silly question. After all, why would anyone want to be poor? And yet it is the destiny of most people in the west to end up poorer than they anticipated.

Let me explain what I mean by the word 'poor'. Clearly there is a difference between struggling to keep up the monthly payments on your Mercedes and the challenges of a subsistence farmer in rural Africa. The definition I would like to use is from *Five Wealth Secrets* by Craig Hill.[3] 'Poor people spend 100% or more of the money they make each month, regardless of how much they earn.' In a recent survey, the American Payroll Association reported that 68% of households would find it 'somewhat difficult or very difficult if their pay checks were delayed by a week'.

I would be very surprised if the figures were much different in the UK. Most people are living very close to the edge financially. There has to be a better way. Robert Kiyosaki, author of *Rich Dad Poor Dad*,[4] asks the question: If you were to give 100 people £10,000 today and told them they could use that money as they wished, what would be the result in a year's time? Apparently eighty of the 100 would have nothing left, sixteen would have between £10,300 and £10,500 and four would have between £20,000 and £1,000,000. Even allowing for some exaggeration and poetic licence, it is true that the vast majority of people don't handle money successfully, while there are a very few who do.

We know this is largely to do with upbringing and the example set by our parents. I will elaborate in a later chapter, but for the moment reflect on how your parents handled money and what they taught you about it as you were growing up, and how that compares with the way you handle your money today. If poverty is having nothing left at the end of the month, prosperity is having enough to give, save and live. It means having no sense of lack but being able to be generous. Prosperity also allows you to fulfil your potential and not be dominated or constrained by your cash flow.

Some of us have a problem with the word 'prosperity'. We think of greedy pastors, tele-evangelists and 'get rich quick' schemes. Let us instead use the word 'abundance'. The core message of this book is that Christians do not need to be poor and are designed to enjoy the abundant life. They can choose to be poor if they want, but it's not part of the plan of God for their lives. I have discovered that abundance is a mixture of right attitudes and right actions. There are still large numbers of Christians, particularly in the UK, who think that being poor is the beginning of holiness. This, as I will attempt to show, is not biblical.

God is a God of extravagance and abundance and loves to bless his children. Blessing covers all areas of life and surely finance must be a part. I recently heard a pastor describe blessing as 'to empower to prosper'. Christians should be leading abundant lives in every respect. They should be wealthy in the fullest meaning of the word. Abundance is not just about having enough money. It's much more than that, it's an abundance of relationships, an abundance of health and an abundance of joy. It's the ability and desire to bless others and to be able to be generous on every occasion. Abundance is enjoying the goodness of God in every area of our lives. It does not mean that you are destined to be a millionaire. Sorry! But it does mean that your life should not be governed by lack or fear.

I want to help you live the life of blessing and generosity God intends for you. This book is in three sections. The first provides the bigger picture of abundance, both from scripture and evidence in the world. The second offers reasons why you may not be prospering currently, and the third is full of practical steps. Please resist any temptation to jump straight to the third section, as a fuller understanding of the background and my reasoning will make this section more beneficial.

So, the question is: Are you living a life which is abundant in all respects or are you sometimes struggling to make ends meet financially?

PART ONE: THE BIG PICTURE

Chapter 1
Abundance from the Beginning

The idea that God is benevolent, kind and generous is backed up by scripture and experience. We will start by exploring the scriptural evidence for a God who wishes to bless his children, starting in Genesis and looking throughout the Hebrew scriptures. This is a whistle-stop tour through the relevant passages, picking out some highlights of God's provision. God is a good God who loves to bless his people, and that includes financial abundance. Poverty is not a blessing from God. This is my starting point, and as we look through the pages of the Bible we can see the goodness and generosity of God displayed.

The Hebrew word *saleah* means to 'succeed' or 'prosper' and it occurs some sixty-five times in the Hebrew scriptures. The word generally expresses the idea of a successful venture, as contrasted with failure. The first use of *saleah* occurs in Genesis 24 verse 21. Here, Abraham's servant is looking for a wife for Isaac and is watching Rebekah to see if she is the one for Isaac and if his journey has been successful. The source of such success is God, as King Uzziah is said to have understood in the book of 2 Chronicles, for 'as long as he sought the Lord, God made him prosper'.[5]

Right at the beginning God gave everything on earth to humankind. He told them to be fruitful and multiply and that everything was under their rulership. The full abundance of creation was under the dominion of the human race. It's clear that abundance and expansion was the original plan. There was nothing which was not given to humankind to enjoy, with the singular exception of the fruit from the tree of good and evil.

Then came the Fall and Adam was told that life would not be as idyllic as it had been. The ground was now cursed and through the sweat of his brow he would have to work the earth all the days of his life in order to eke out a living. That seems to have been the lot of most of humankind since then. The biblical exceptions I quote below are of those who sought to follow God and live according to his ways. Scripture shows us that God had provided a bountiful earth with riches for everyone. The first mention of gold is in Genesis 2 verses 11 to 12: the river flowing from Eden through the land of Havilah is mentioned, 'where there is gold. (The gold of that land is good;).'[6] Right at the beginning we can see an indication that gold has value.

God provided abundantly the large quantities of the right kind of wood that Noah needed to build his Ark. The patriarchs, Abraham, Isaac and Jacob, became very wealthy and it was clear this was owing to the blessing of God. By the time Abraham went to rescue his nephew Lot who had been kidnapped, he had 318 trained men in his household.[7] He must have been very wealthy to support a household of that size. Isaac became rich and the Bible says that his wealth continued to grow until he became very wealthy.[8] It is clear that God's blessing of Isaac was also related to his obedience. God told him not to leave the land in a time of famine but to plant crops where he was instead, and he received a bumper harvest!

Isaac's son, Jacob, had nothing when he had to flee to his uncle Laban after he cheated his brother. He later returned with wives, children, flocks and herds. On his way to Laban's house he had a dream in which God told him that he and his descendants would own the land he was lying on, and not only be blessed but be a blessing to all the peoples on earth. In response, always the wheeler dealer, he offered God ten per cent of anything God gave him,[9] presumably by way of sacrificial offerings. In a later encounter with an angel, Jacob had his name changed to Israel. Jacob eventually produces twelve sons, which became the twelve tribes known as the 'children of Israel'. Thus God had fulfilled his promise; not only had the Jewish people been a blessing to the world, but they also were chosen to host the Messiah.

Joseph, Jacob's eleventh son, relying on wisdom from God, became very wealthy as assistant to Pharaoh. He saved a nation from starvation and was able to look after all his family in a time of famine. When the time was right for the children of Israel to leave Egypt, God provided a truly great (and modest) leader in Moses. After the exodus, God provided food and water for his people during their desert wanderings, on their way to their new homeland. As they approached the land of Canaan, twelve spies were sent to check if it really was a land of promise. When the spies returned from their initial foray into Canaan, they described it as a land flowing with milk and honey and brought back the world's largest bunch of grapes (Numbers 13:23). Despite the disobedience of the people who failed, through fear of the indigenous peoples, to go up and take the land, God still provided food daily and clothing which didn't wear out for the following 39 years, until the next generation was ready to occupy the Promised Land. Thus, the principle of abundance is found in the Torah, which comprises the five books of Moses: Genesis, Exodus, Leviticus, Numbers and Deuteronomy. (The word *torah* is usually wrongly translated as 'law' but actually means 'teaching' or 'instruction'; it is God's original blueprint for life.) Moses taught the people to remember the Lord their God, for it is he who gives them 'the ability to produce wealth, and so confirms his covenant, which he swore to [their] ancestors, as it is today'.[10] There was no doubt in Moses' mind that the ability to generate wealth was evidence that God had chosen the Israelites as his special people. In Deuteronomy 15:4-5 we read: 'However, there should not be any poor among you, for the Lord will surely bless you in the land that he is giving you as an inheritance, if you carefully obey him by keeping all these commandments that I am giving you today.'

God instructed Moses to tell Aaron how, as the high priest, he should bless the people. 'The Lord bless you and keep you; The Lord make his face shine on you and be gracious to you; The Lord turn his face towards you and give you peace' (Num. 6:24-26). That blessing included wellbeing, protection and peace. The word for peace in Hebrew is *shalom,* which means much more than an absence of strife. It includes wholeness, completeness, prosperity and tranquility. That blessing is for all of us. And, having said that there should be no poor amongst them, in the next verses in Deuteronomy 15 God instructs the Israelites to be generous to poor people. 'If anyone is poor among your fellow Israelites in any of the towns of the land that the Lord your God is giving you, do not be hard-hearted or tight-fisted towards them. Rather be open-handed and freely lend them whatever they need'. We can conclude that a life of abundance is available to all but is not automatic or universal, even though God has said there should be no poor among us. Deuteronomy 28 lists all the blessings that would follow obeying God and all the curses which would come from disobedience. It's clear from this passage that following God leads to abundance, and disobedience leads to being cursed rather than blessed. However, we shouldn't conclude that the reason some people are poor is because they are cursed as a result of disobedience.

There are many paths that can lead to poverty, and disobedience to God's direction is simply one of them.

After Moses came Joshua, and the conquering of the land flowing with milk and honey. Then came the days of the Judges, where the nation seesawed between peaceful prosperity and afflicted famine. This was clearly the outworking of Deuteronomy 28, as the people sometimes followed God, and were blessed, and at other times the local pagan gods, and were anything but blessed.

The monarchy, which followed this time, brought a measure of cohesion to the nation as King David, and then his son Solomon, took wealth to a new level. David is called a man after God's heart, and God gave him great success in battle and conquest. He wrote many psalms of gratitude to God for his prosperity, and that of his nation. Solomon was one of the wealthiest people who ever lived. He was blessed by God because he desired to put his responsibilities as king before personal gain. When God appeared to him in a dream and told him he could ask for anything he wanted, he humbled himself and asked God for wisdom to govern his people. God was so pleased at his request that he gave him honour and wealth to go with it. Solomon was, for most of his reign, a great blessing to the nation: 'The people of Judah and Israel were as numerous as the sand on the seashore; they ate, they drank and they were happy' (1 Kings 4:20). He passed on his wisdom by writing most of the book of Proverbs.

Proverbs has a lot to say about money: how to get it, be generous with it, not trust in it, and how wisdom is to be pursued rather than wealth. If wisdom comes, wealth will follow. In all, there are over 100 proverbs which talk about money. The book of Proverbs warns against letting the desire for riches become greater than the desire for wisdom. With wisdom will come abundance but chasing after money will lead to disaster. The point is conclusively made in the book that seeking to follow God brings peace and prosperity.

As Solomon aged, things went somewhat awry. In later life he wrote the book of Ecclesiastes, where he takes stock of the mysteries and enigmas of life. He discovers that human wisdom has its limits. He concludes that a life not centred on God is purposeless and meaningless. Without him nothing else can satisfy. With him is life in its fullness, and all the gifts of God are to be gratefully received and enjoyed. Ecclesiastes has lots to say about wealth and the human condition. It says that those who love money will never have enough, and that the secret of happiness is in being content with your circumstances.

After Solomon's death the kingdom was divided and never regained the glory of his day. It reverted to the seesaw of being in and out of favour with God. The people would fall away and worship the local deities. As they disobeyed the word of God, so the negative effects of Deuteronomy 28 were felt as either famine or oppression resulted. Eventually the Israelites would realise the error of their ways and turn back to God, after the prophets admonished Israel for turning to foreign gods and neglecting the worship of the one true God.

Time and time again, Israel would be punished by famine or occupation by a foreign power when they were disobedient. This pattern continued until the time of Jesus, when Rome was the occupying power. In other words, what we have seen demonstrated throughout the Old Testament is that turning from God will bring poverty, not always immediately but there will be trouble sooner or later. Turning back to God in repentance would reverse the curse and open the floodgates of heaven's provision again.

From this study, we can see clearly that God has blessed the earth with abundance. The human race is to enjoy that abundance with gratitude to the Lord who has supplied it. It is a command that we remembering poor and needy people; those who do so will be blessed. Serving other gods or running after riches may appear to work in the short term but eventually will always lead to disaster. Those who follow the Lord and obey his commands will prosper and be blessed.

Reflect on some of the Old Testament passages for yourself and see if you come to the same conclusion.

work in the short term, but eventually will show . . . lead to . . . quarrel. Those who will be in the lead in their . . . commands will . . . peace, and be blessed.

Reflection: see ... of the Old Testament passages for yourself and see if you understand the same conclusion.

Chapter 2
What About the New Testament?

The New Testament also has plenty to say about money. There are clearly spiritual blessings in Jesus, and I believe these are in addition to the material blessings of the Old Testament, rather than a replacement for them. After all, Jesus was brought up as a Jew and would have been familiar with the Hebrew scriptures. He would have known very well that obedience led to abundance. Surely the new covenant is supposed to be better than the old, so why would the new covenant lead to less abundance on any level?

We see both wealth and poverty demonstrated in the life of Jesus. He was born into a family which would have been the equivalent of middle class today. Joseph, his earthly father, was a carpenter, a skilled tradesman. There was probably some money in the family as Joseph of Arimathea, who later gave Jesus his burial place, was thought to be the uncle of his mother, Mary, and a wealthy man.

Jesus was born and placed in a manger, not because his parents could not afford a room, but because the inns were full. There is some evidence for Jesus' origins being modest in that when he was dedicated at the Temple at forty days old, the offerings presented by Joseph and Mary were a pair of doves rather than the lamb and a dove, which wealthier people would have given. However, he did not stay poor. His visitors were rich and poor, but the Magi (the three kings), who probably visited around a year after his birth, brought some pretty expensive gifts with them. The Bible does not tell us how much gold, frankincense and myrrh were brought, but all are extremely valuable and precious commodities. In today's terms this could have been worth many tens of thousands of pounds. Certainly enough to finance the family's flight to Egypt,[11] and then to support themselves before returning to Israel some years later.

Whether you picture Jesus as rich or poor depends on which side of the cross you are looking. You can view Jesus as the poor suffering servant with nowhere to lay his head, or you can see him as the resurrected, glorified superhero, seated at the right hand of his Father, enjoying the riches of heaven. Paul, writing to the Corinthian church, says, 'For you know the grace of our Lord Jesus Christ, that though he was rich, yet for your sake he became poor, so that you through his poverty might become rich'.[12] He became poor for us, so we do not have to wear the mantle of poverty.

Jesus' first sermon,[13] quoting from Isaiah 61, begins with the fact that he is bringing good news to those who are poor. What would poor people consider to be good news? Surely, it's the fact that in future they could be less poor! (I accept there are spiritual implications, as in 'poor in spirit', but I believe this includes the material meaning.) Jesus spoke more about money and material possessions than anything else. Nowhere does he suggest that wealth is a bad thing in itself. He certainly does say that wealth is a bad thing if it causes you to run after it and put the acquisition of money before anything else. But he demonstrated abundance wherever he went: for example, in large catches of fish, food for 5,000 or fine wine for a wedding. He also brought healing and deliverance to all who came to him.

Jesus' first miracle at the wedding in Cana[14] exemplifies his abundant approach. As the wine had run out, he changed six stone jars full of water into the best wine. Those jars held between twenty and thirty gallons each. So, assuming they held twenty-five gallons each, six of them would have contained 150 gallons of wine. This is the equivalent of 900 standard wine bottles! That would have been quite a celebration. Wherever he went Jesus demonstrated abundant generosity to those who came to him. Whether they came for healing or to hear his message, they left fulfilled. As his ministry grew, he attracted wealthy followers who supported him and presumably the disciples as well.

The Gospels contain many examples of Jesus' views on generosity and abundance. When the disciples were instructed to give the large crowd something to eat, they protested that spending more than half a year's wages, which might be equivalent to about £12,000 today, seemed excessive. There was no suggestion that they did not have that amount of money with them, only that it seemed a lot to spend at once. [15]Then he fed the 5,000 men, besides women and children; they all ate their fill and there were twelve baskets of leftovers. No one went hungry. A second time he fed 4,000 men, besides women and children, as he saw they were in a remote place and were hungry.[16] Whenever Jesus went fishing the catch was so abundant as to be net-bursting, as in Luke 5. In the Sermon on the Mount,[17] Jesus was clear that those who seek first the kingdom and his righteousness will have all else added to them. He taught us to pray for our daily bread and not to worry about it. Jesus also taught that we should never serve money (mammon) and God as no one can have two masters, but we are to serve God and he would take care of us. Money was something that we have and use, and we must be careful never to let money have and use us. The old English word 'mammon' is used to denote the spirit behind money. It implies excessive materialism, greed, and unjust worldly gain.

The story of the rich young ruler, often used to exemplify why we should avoid prosperity, shows that he was over-attached to his wealth.[18] Nowhere else does Jesus tell anyone to sell everything and give it away. Jesus did say here, though, that it was difficult for a rich person to get into the kingdom of heaven, as difficult as squeezing a camel through the eye of a needle. This statement clearly shocked the disciples, but Jesus went on to say that 'what is impossible with man is possible with God'. The common belief at the time was that wealth was evidence of God's approval, and Jesus was using a figure of speech to make his point. I believe this passage is saying that those who rely on wealth to get into heaven will be disappointed as only the grace of God will let us in.

Jesus enjoyed the company of rich and poor alike. Indeed, Jesus had financial support from a number of women from their own resources.[19] As the disciples went from place to place Jesus assigned a designated treasurer to look after their money (Judas), implying that they travelled with money. When he taught about stewardship in the parable of the talents,[20] Jesus praised those who had doubled their cash. He admonished the servant who was too scared to invest and just hid his money out of fear. This shows that good stewardship is more about generating wealth than merely conserving it. Jesus left the riches of heaven to bring them to us. He seemed to become poor in material terms, but he was never constrained by a lack of finance.

The rest of the New Testament does not say much about money, more about not being greedy and about having generous hearts. Generosity is a key theme with the early believers, who held everything in common and ensured there were no needy people among them (Acts 2:44-45). From the letters of Paul, it's clear that blessing will follow acts of generous and cheerful giving. It's the love of money which is the root of all evil rather than money itself.

Paul is very concerned for the salvation of the Jewish people.[21] In Romans 10 verse 19, he quotes Moses addressing the Israelites knowing that they would fall away and follow false gods. 'I will make you envious by those who are not a nation,' he says, meaning that the Jews will become jealous of the Gentiles because they have a relationship with God which seems much better than that which the Jews have. Now what is that better relationship going to look like, in order to make Jewish people jealous? I propose that it certainly would not have been one based on poverty!

The book of James is full of practical wisdom about faith and works, particularly admonishing rich oppressors, and the effects of greed and selfishness. Yet James 4 verse 2 tells us that 'you do not have because you do not ask God,' reminding us that he is the provider of everything we need. James goes on, in verse 3, to tell us that although it's fine to ask God for needs and even our desires, if we are asking with wrong motives, such as self-indulgence, then we should not expect a positive response. Again, we are reminded that the state of our hearts has an impact on what we receive.

Finally, there is a verse which has been used and misused by so many prosperity teachers. However, I believe that it really does encourage abundance on all levels: 'I pray that you may prosper in every way and be in good health physically just as you are spiritually.'[22] It seems clear to me that the Bible does not teach that having money is bad, provided that it is not taking the place of God in our lives and becomes an obsession, and provided that we use our money wisely and are generous to others.

Does the Bible allow me to want more money?

It's fine to want more money if you do not have enough to feed and clothe yourself or your family properly and you are not able to save for the future. It's also fine if you want more to bless others and use it for godly purposes (seeking first his kingdom). It's not fine to want more money simply so you can have more possessions or because you think that greater wealth equals greater security. I recently heard about one couple who had so much in the way of possessions that they decided to move to a bigger house with a double garage so they would have enough room for storage! That does not sound like the right attitude to me.

The book of Revelation describes the New Jerusalem coming down from heaven as a city literally made of gold and precious stones. We are told to pray 'on earth as it is in heaven'. God surely would not use images of valuable things in heaven if wealth was inherently bad or we were not to expect quality things on earth.

If you truly delight in the Lord and put his kingdom agenda first, then he will bless you. As I have studied these verses over the years, I have come to the conclusion that good things come to believers, sooner or later, by expectant faith.

Read Matthew 6 verses 19-34 and reflect on God's provision for you.

Chapter 3
Poverty and Holiness

There is a commonly held belief that a lack of material goods is necessary for holiness. Yet, as we have read in the Bible passages so far, wealth is seen as a good thing. Proverbs 10 verse 22 says: 'The blessing of the Lord brings wealth, without painful toil for it'. The biblical writers leave no doubt that the wealth of the patriarchs was a sign of God's favour. However, those who are wealthy are warned not to exploit others; they must pay their workers properly and on time. Poverty is never considered in a positive light, and rich people are charged with helping those who are poor and not oppressing or exploiting them, which brought admonishment from the prophets.

Jesus came and was acutely aware of the needs of poor people. He told the rich young ruler to sell all he had and give it to those who were poor.[23] In the New Testament, there is greater emphasis on helping the brethren in need and those who are poor. But nowhere does Jesus suggest that poverty is a good thing in itself or something to aspire to. In Luke 6 verses 20-26, he addresses those who are poor and hungry on a much deeper level than the physical, and encourages them to rejoice that they will receive great reward in heaven. He goes on to warn those who are rich and carefree, who seek only material blessings and status. Money can dull our appetite for God and the spiritual life.

Paul writes to the Corinthian church: 'For you know the grace of our Lord Jesus Christ, that though he was rich, yet for your sake he became poor, so that you through his poverty might become rich'.[24] But he writes this in the context of them being generous givers, to help alleviate others' poverty.

To be holy is to live a life set apart for God. We are declared righteous by accepting Christ as our saviour, which is the first step to holiness.[25] To lead a holy life means obeying God's word and living accordingly, resisting sin and sexual immorality and separating ourselves from evil. Arguably this may be easier to do if you are poor, as many of the world's temptations are out of reach and lack can mean enforced purity and simplicity of life. Poverty, though, can also lead to other temptations, such as theft or prostitution, in order to survive. The strength to stay pure only comes through the power of the Holy Spirit dwelling within us. Unfortunately, the Church through the ages has emphasised both poverty and holiness as the way to salvation. Living a holy life is a demonstration of Jesus dwelling within, not a work to gain his favour.

How did the idea that poverty was a prerequisite for holiness take root? The Early Church was seen as a sect of Judaism, as all the earliest disciples were Jewish. Their outlook would have been framed by the Hebrew scriptures. They were known as followers of 'the Way' within Judaism and not as a separate religion. As the Church grew, Gentiles (non-Jews) became believers and the influence of Judaism lessened. Nevertheless, the Early Church would have carried on celebrating the Jewish festivals.

The idea that poverty was essential for holiness seems to have originated with the early Christians known as the Desert Fathers and Mothers. These devoted men and women lived in the deserts of

Arabia, usually as hermits or in small communities (monasteries) to escape the wicked ways of the world and focus on God.

St Augustine of Hippo (354-430) codified monastic life. He had lived a hedonistic lifestyle as a youth and, upon converting to Christianity at the age of thirty-one, he soon became a priest and then a bishop. He wrote over 100 separate titles on all aspects of Christian doctrine. He embraced the monastic lifestyle of celibacy and poverty.

St Benedict of Nursia (480-547) is known as the 'father of western monasticism'. He studied in Rome but became so upset by the immorality of society there that he left and spent some years in a cave seeking God. His piety became known and he attracted disciples. He founded several monasteries (Benedictines) and wrote the *Rule of St Benedict*.

St Francis of Assisi (1191-1226) was also from a wealthy background. He had a conversion experience and embraced the life of a penitent, giving away his possessions and renouncing his inheritance.

The early believers were influenced by the cultural shift which gradually occurred in the Church from that of a Hebrew mindset to a Greek way of thinking. Plato, the Greek philosopher, introduced the idea of the dualism of humankind, which held that the soul was good but the flesh always evil. This has led to the spiritual-secular divide, where the kingdom of God is something which happens in church on Sunday and has little impact on the other days of the week, particularly on the secular world of work. This is in direct contrast to the ancient Hebrew way of thinking, which saw humans as a whole being with God ruling in every facet of life. Everything in that culture was part of worship and was to be done 'as unto the Lord'.

The distinction between Greek and Hebrew ways of thinking influences much more of our lives than we may realise. We read our

Hebraically written Bibles from a perspective that's been conditioned by our education, one which is steeped in westernised Greek thought patterns. Yet there are notable differences: the Hebrew is concerned with action and practice, the Greek with thought and knowledge; right conduct is the ultimate concern of the Hebrew, right thinking that of the Greek; and the Hebrew extols moral virtue as the substance of life, whereas the Greek subordinates practical matters to intellectual virtues.

For about the first 200 years the Early Church was composed largely of Jewish believers. However, as the number of Gentiles increased and the effects of the surrounding culture permeated the Church, so it succumbed to much of the Hellenistic (Greek) approach to life.

The Roman emperor Constantine (who ruled from 306 to 337) recognised that the Church was flourishing and growing at what seemed to him an alarming pace. He knew he had to have the Church on his side as emperor, having seen that persecution of the Church by his predecessors only served to increase the number of believers. So, he converted to Christianity, and started to take control of the Church, declaring himself its head. He began to blend the Church calendar with the pagan one and separate it from its Jewish roots. He hated the Jews, whom he saw as a rebellious and troublesome bunch. The Sabbath day of rest became Sunday, the day of the sun god. He instituted Easter named after the pagan fertility goddess Eostre (meaning spring), instead of Passover, and celebrated the Nativity on the birthday of the sun; the winter solstice, 25 December. In fact, Constantine did as much as he could to separate the Church from Judaism and blend it with paganism. And from the fourth century onwards, the Church moved increasingly further from its Hebrew roots.

As a result, instead of all of life being considered spiritual and 'as unto the Lord', including making money, the focus shifted to viewing the inner, contemplative life as much more holy than that of the everyday. Some wanted to separate themselves entirely from worldly temptations and this led to the rise of monastic communities and the division between clergy and laity.

The monastic community became the example of holiness. Men and women who had given up the idea of personal possessions for a life of simplicity and prayer, away from the temptations around them. It does seem paradoxical that through the Middle Ages and onwards, while monks and nuns were living lives of voluntary poverty, the Church, represented by the Vatican, was growing richer and richer. It's thought that the Church in medieval times owned twenty to thirty per cent of the land in Western Europe, in an era when land was the primary form of wealth. The corruption and wealth of the Church hierarchy was one of the causes of the Protestant Reformation.

Monastic communities were known for good works, hospitality and caring for those who were sick. Christians need to continue to serve in these ways, but not to withdraw from the world, I believe. We are allowed to enjoy the material blessings of life as long as we share them and are not driven or dominated by them. For the monks and nuns, poverty was seen as a blessing; for most of us it is a curse. While 'the love of money is a root of all kinds of evil',[26] a lack of money can be the cause of all sorts of trouble for us. According to Professor David Miller of Princeton University, Protestant Christianity has had three prevalent attitudes towards wealth. He states that Protestants have variously viewed wealth as an offence to the Christian faith, an obstacle to faith, and the outcome of faith.[27] Today we can see all three attitudes at work. There are those who believe that Christians should keep nothing for themselves beyond the basic necessities of life and give everything else away; that because Jesus became poor, we should be like him. Martin Luther viewed the desire for wealth as 'the most common idol on earth', and quoted the parable of the rich young ruler[28] as an example of wealth as an obstacle to faith. And Jesus taught very clearly that *pursuing* wealth was a diversion, leading away from the kingdom of God.

Is prosperity the outcome of faith? It certainly was for the patriarchs of the Old Testament. Consequently, we who live under a new and better covenant can expect to live a life which is abundant in every way. The challenge for us is the wise use of that abundance.

Dallas Willard wrote: 'The idealization of poverty is one of the most dangerous illusions of Christians in the contemporary world. Stewardship which requires possessions and includes giving is the true spiritual discipline in relation to wealth.'[29]

Take time to reflect on your own attitudes towards wealth and poverty.

Chapter 4
Is There Enough To Go Around?

Thinking about our own prosperity can raise questions about others' wealth, or lack of it. At times I've found myself wondering if I deserve to be prosperous, and whether it is possible to be prosperous without taking from others. You may also have wondered whether there is enough wealth to go around, or if your financial health means someone else has to go without. There is a school of thought that believes that the amount of wealth in the world is finite and that you can't have more without someone else having less. This would seem a reasonable and, indeed, a likely scenario as we see a rise in global population and wonder how we will all be fed. In reality, however, this could not be further from the truth.

God has gifted humankind with resourcefulness and imagination which has brought ever greater prosperity to the world. Our God is a creative God and new sources of wealth are being created or discovered almost every day. The technological revolution we are currently enjoying means that new businesses are started, which leads to more employment. Many goods are becoming cheaper. I went to buy a new television recently and was astounded by the improvement in quality, and that the price for a screen about twice the size was about half the amount I paid for my old one ten years ago! I realise that this is a western-world example, but the world overall is getting richer. Professor Hans Rosling, an expert in international health, has clearly demonstrated that standards of living are rising across the earth and the numbers of people globally in extreme poverty have fallen substantially over the past 200 years. (Have a look at his brief but enlightening YouTube presentation, entitled '200 countries, 200 years, 4 minutes - The Joy of Stats – BBC Four.')

Things are getting better globally, and in most cases this benefits those who are poor. Increases in solar and wind energy generation, along with improved battery storage technology, will radically improve air quality. Real wealth is being created from non-polluting sources; genuine wealth creation. I am not suggesting that all is perfect, or that there are not some exploitative companies, but that does not mean that all business is bad, all companies are just after your money or that everybody wants to get rich at your expense.

You may be thinking that the earth is only so big, that populations are increasing, and that we must surely start to use up resources in the near future. The idea that we must be running out came from a group called the Club of Rome. Founded in 1968, it consists of current and former heads of state, UN bureaucrats and high-level politicians, along with scientists and some business leaders. They began to be concerned with the future of the world and commissioned a report from the Massachusetts Institute of Technology to look into how the five variables of 'population, food production, industrialisation, pollution and consumption of non-renewable natural resources interacted'. They concluded that if population growth continued at its current rate, many items would run out over the next 100 years. They also concluded that if there were no new discoveries oil would run out by 1992![30]

The Population Bomb, written by Paul and Anne Ehrlich[31] in 1968, became a bestseller. This book warned of mass starvation in the 1970s and 1980s owing to overpopulation, as well as other major societal upheavals, and advocated immediate action to limit population growth. This can all seem very logical. The earth appears to have limited natural resources and, as more and more people consume at western levels, we must eventually start to run out of the raw materials to create wealth. This is a view shared by many scientists, but it ignores human ingenuity. It assumes that populations keep increasing and that we all continue to use the same raw materials in ever-increasing quantities. The belief that some necessities of life will run out soon takes no account of the fact that what was a necessity in 1968 has been superseded by new materials fifty years later. For example, coal and oil powered most things in 1968; today, electricity from solar and wind energy is gradually replacing them.

Julian Simon was a professor of economic theory at the University of Maryland who published a book in 1981[32] that criticised the conventional wisdom on resource scarcity. His theory was that scarcity would increase the cost of a product, thus creating the incentive to find alternative materials. So convinced was Simon that he challenged Paul Ehrlich to a bet. He wagered $10,000 that five raw materials of Ehrlich's choice would fall in price over the next ten years, rather than rise. Ehrlich agreed the wager and he chose copper, chromium, nickel, tin and tungsten. Ehrlich lost the bet. Now here's the point: Simon's work was updated in a 2018 study[33] of the price of fifty global commodities between 1980 and 2018. Real prices fell by an average of thirty-six per cent, despite global population increasing by sixty-nine per cent over the same period. A more accurate way to assess the cost to people of these commodities is to calculate their 'time price': the amount of time an average person must work to earn enough to buy them. On that basis, the cost of these commodities fell much further by a whopping seventy-two per cent. If it took sixty minutes of work to buy this notional basket of commodities in 1980, it only took sixteen point six minutes of work to afford them in 2018. If that trend continued, the price of these resources would halve every twenty-one years.

This study, by Pooley and Tupy at the Cato Institute, Washington DC, even came up with an 'abundance index' which demonstrates that the earth is 519.98% more abundant in 2018 than it was in 1980. How does this make sense physically, on a planet of notionally fixed resources? The researchers came up with a beautiful analogy: 'The world is a closed system in the way that a piano is a closed system. The instrument has only 88 notes, but those notes can be played in a nearly infinite variety of ways ...The Earth's atoms may be fixed, but the possible combinations of those atoms are infinite. What matters, then, is not the physical limits of our planet, but human freedom to experiment and reimagine the use of resources that we have.' As Hans Rowling and Julian Simon have shown, humanity is becoming more prosperous and we will not be running out of resources anytime soon.

As I write, the world is experiencing the COVID-19 pandemic which is causing substantial economic paralysis almost everywhere. It's tempting, currently, to allow fear to rule and believe that the end of civilisation as we know it is upon us. I am confident that by the time you read this book, a combination of human ingenuity and the effect of mass prayer will have brought about recovery and a return to normality.

Even the spectre of global populations increasing to the point of unsustainability seems very unlikely. Human beings are the only species on earth where an abundance of resources leads to lower birth rates. In a 2018 study by Deutsche Bank[34] quoted by Daniel Hannan in the *Telegraph* (6 August 2019), the counter-intuitive truth is argued that we are heading, sooner or later, for depopulation. The study suggests that global population will reach 8.7 billion in

2055 before dropping back to 8 billion by the end of the century. As global wealth increases, and infant mortality declines, in every continent economic development is squeezing fertility. The rate of reproduction in Kenya has fallen over the past fifty years from 8 live births per woman to 3.5. In Iran, the decline is 6.8 to 2.1; in Brazil, 5.7 to 1.7. The wealthier the country, the deeper the drop. In richer developed countries, the birth rate is far below replacement level: ranging from Germany at 1.6, to South Korea at 1.1.

This still leaves us with the challenge of managing the natural world as good stewards. Here again, human ingenuity will always find a way. The world is waking up to the dangers of pollution both by vehicle emissions and plastic litter, and is taking action. Although it still remains to be seen how humanity will rise to the challenge of climate change, there is a groundswell of global public opinion which is demanding that governments address the issue. Much new technology is being focused on solving these challenges. Recently I invested in a company which plans to turn domestic waste into aviation fuel. I remain optimistic for the future. It is true that the global response to protecting the planet is patchy; we see tropical forests still being cleared for grazing land, and increased amounts of polluting carbon dioxide being emitted in the developing world. At the same time, however, we see trees being planted and a rapid increase in the uptake of alternative energy and recycling schemes. In Ethiopia a campaign to plant 4 billion trees has started, with what must be a world record of over 353 million being planted in one 12-hour period. God has given us an abundant planet; we have a responsibility to steward it well.

I am growing more of my own vegetables and cutting down on meat consumption, refilling our reusable water bottle from the tap and consciously trying to buy less plastic. If we each do our part then we can, with a clear conscience, prosper and enjoy the bounty of this planet without it reducing what is available to others.

Some see capitalism as the problem, others see it as the solution. To explore capitalism as against socialism or communism is well beyond the scope of this book! All I would say is that business practices do not need to be exploitative. There are those who prosper at the expense of others. Fraudsters, con artists, rogue traders, thieves and scammers all take from others and leave them poorer. There are some companies who prosper for a time by paying their workers badly. For reputable, ethical businesses the reverse is true. They prosper by providing services of value, and treating their staff well. They make money by meeting needs and helping others achieve their objectives.

If I pay a cleaner or a gardener to provide a service for me, they are doing something for me which I do not wish to or cannot do myself. They are not exploiting me. I am rewarding those who give me value. As long as I am paying a fair wage then I am blessing them by providing employment, not exploiting them. Quality of service is more important to the success of a business than almost any other factor. We live in an age of customer reviews which can make or break a business. Ask any restaurant owner! Most of my working life has been in business as a financial adviser. My aim was that my clients should be grateful they met me as my service to them increased their wealth and helped them realise their dreams. It has been my objective that my client should always profit more from our transactions than I did, with the effect that both they and I have been blessed. We may sometimes feel exploited by our energy suppliers or our mobile phone operators, but in our economic system, though it is far from perfect, competition arises, and new entrants come into the market, undercutting the established operators or offering a better service. Nobody can make money for long without providing fair value.

You are worthy

Many people feel distinctly unworthy of blessing and of course we are only worthy because of the cross. Jesus took our sin upon himself and opened up the way to relationship with the Father. It can sometimes feel much easier to understand how others deserve to be blessed rather than ourselves. Perhaps we reason that they are kinder, better-looking or more loveable than we are. But according to Acts 10:34, God is no respecter of persons. We are all his favourites!

Through the parable of the prodigal son, in Luke 15, Jesus illustrates how many of us have behaved towards God. The younger son of a wealthy farmer effectively wished his father dead so he could inherit his share and go off and live the high life. Yet his father couldn't wait for his eventual return, even though the son had wasted all his inheritance. As the son approaches, his father throws the best robe round him and puts the choicest food on the table. In the same way, the Father throws his robe of righteousness around us as we approach him. He declares us worthy of blessing, because he loves us as his sons and daughters.

In 1 Chronicles chapter 4 we come across a character called Jabez. He is only mentioned once in the Bible and he didn't have a very good start in life. His mother named him Jabez, which means 'sorrowful' or 'sorrow maker', because of her pain in labour. But he was of good character; he was 'more honourable than his brothers'. We read that Jabez 'cried out to the God of Israel'. He knew who he was speaking to and the phrase 'cried out' implies fervent prayer. He prays: 'Oh, that you would bless me and enlarge my territory!' He was not afraid to ask for increase and prosperity, fervently and energetically! He continues: 'Let your hand be with me, and keep me from harm so that I will be free from pain'. Jabez asks too for protection and health, 'And God granted his request'.

It's worth lingering here for a while until you are fully convinced of who you are in Christ. This is because we need to recognise that we now have the Holy Spirit living inside us. We are seated in heavenly places in Christ.[35] We have a Heavenly Father who owns the cattle on a thousand hills,[36] we are not just his heirs but his beloved sons and daughters, adopted into his family. He delights in blessing us. All the promises of the old covenant are available to those in Christ. All the blessings of Deuteronomy 28 are available to those who would believe that Jesus is the Messiah. These blessings come upon your family, your storehouses and on everything to which you put your hands.

Many of us somehow find it much easier to believe in an eternity of delight in heaven than for blessing in the here and now. Many Christians are more readily disposed to 'take up their cross and follow me.'[37] They expect a life of persecution and suffering for their faith. However, we read in Mark 10 verses 29-30: 'Truly I tell you,' Jesus replied, 'no one who has left home or brothers or sisters or mother or father or children or fields for me and the gospel will fail to receive a hundred times as much in this present age … and in the age to come eternal life.'

You are a new creation: 2 Corinthians 5 verses 17-18 state, 'Therefore, if anyone is in Christ, the new creation has come: the old has gone, the new is here! All this is from God, who reconciled us to himself through Christ and gave us the ministry of reconciliation.' Our old negative selves have gone, and we are now seated with Christ in heavenly places. We still must 'count ourselves dead to sin'[38] so we do not slip back into our old attitudes. You are a son or daughter of the King of kings. Just as my children when they were young would expect that their father would provide abundantly for their needs, so you can expect the Lord to have good things for you. He says in Matthew 7:

Ask and it will be given to you; seek and you will find; knock and the door will be opened to you. For everyone who asks receives; the one who seeks finds; and to the one who knocks, the door will be opened. Which of you, if your son asks for bread, will give him a stone? Or if he asks for a fish, will give him a snake? If you, then, though you are evil, know how to give good gifts to your children, how much more will your Father in heaven give good gifts to those who ask him! (Matthew 7:7-11)

I remember the look on my eldest son's face when I was able to buy him a brand new bicycle when all his previous ones had been second hand. It gave me so much pleasure to bless him and I believe that is just a faint reflection of how our Heavenly Father delights in blessing us.

You are the one who God loves, not just the person next to you, but you. He so loved the world that he sent his Son to rescue us. Experiencing his abundance comes by faith, which means believing that the God who made heaven and earth sent his Son to die for you. If you don't believe that, then this book may not make a lot of sense and I suggest that you put it down, find a quiet place and ask God to reveal himself to you, then go and find a Christian and ask them about their faith.

If you are a believer, do you really believe that God loves you enough to want you to have a life of abundance?

Chapter 5
What About Poor People?

Jesus said that 'the poor you will always have with you'.[39] It would seem we can always expect that there will be some poor people. That is why the Hebrew scriptures stress generosity, with instructions such as not harvesting fields right to the boundaries, and not gathering any grapes that have dropped in the vineyard so that some is left for those who need it.[40]

All through the Old Testament concern is raised for poor people. Jesus' heart for them is evidenced, as we've seen, in his first sermon, when he quotes from Isaiah 61: he's bringing 'good news to the poor'. It would be easy to assume that Jesus considered being rich as sin; we have seen that he tells the rich young ruler to sell everything and give it to those who are poor.[41] This has been interpreted by some commentators to mean that all of us should give all our wealth away to poor people. Yet, as we saw in Chapter 2, this is the only example where Jesus tells someone to give everything away and, as is clear from the text, possessions were more important to this young man than anything else. It's a lesson that the kingdom must come first. If wealth is more important to us, then we don't have money - it has us! At other times Jesus ate with wealthy people, particularly tax collectors, but does not tell them to give everything away. His very presence is enough to make cheats such as Zacchaeus repent and make amends.

Jesus was also happy to enjoy the generosity of those who were wealthy. As he travelled around ministering to all, he had not only his twelve close disciples but also a number of women who had been healed and some who were wealthy. 'These women were helping to support them out of their own means'.[42] Possibly out of gratitude for their healing, but more likely because they had found a cause worth supporting.

Jesus made Judas the treasurer of the group to expose his heart, which was more interested in money than the kingdom. In his great wisdom God used the betrayal by Judas for the greater good as it led to Jesus' crucifixion and resurrection, taking our sin and setting us free. Sadly, his betrayal has been used down the centuries to justify antisemitism.

Jesus uses money as a picture in the parable of the talents.[43] He praises the servants who increased their resources and admonishes the one who just kept the money safe. This parable is really about all the talents which we have been blessed with and how we need to put them to good use. Nevertheless, I don't believe Jesus would have used an example like this if he disapproved of making money.

Clearly there are places in the world where Christians are hungry, where there is just not enough food for everyone. Famine is always the result of misused wealth. In the Bible, famine was usually a punishment for turning away from God and worshiping idols or attributing fertility and abundance to the pagan gods of the land. Today, famine can usually be traced back to conflict situations, which lead to the displacement of people who can then no longer work their lands. Climate change plays an increasing part, making the results of conflict worse. We do live in a fallen world and Christians are not immune from the actions of governments and the misuse of resources by rulers.

If the gospel really works and God's desire really is to bless us, there should be evidence in the developing world of what a transformed, abundant, living community looks like. In fact, there are a number of communities around the world that have been changed, sometimes dramatically, by the response of believers to the Holy Spirit. An article in *Renewal Journal* (April 2014)[44] records the following examples.

Mizoram, North-East India

There are approximately 750,000 people living in the region of Mizoram in north-east India. The first Christian missionaries arrived in 1884. The result is that approximately ninety per cent of the region's population are now Christians. The article states that in 120 years the local tribes have gone 'from being a fierce head-hunting society to a model community - and quite possibly the most thoroughly Christian place of comparable size on earth. Certainly, in India there is no other city or state can lay claim to having no homeless people, no beggars, no starvation and 100 percent literacy.'

When this report was written, the churches of Mizoram were sending about a thousand missionaries to the surrounding regions of India and beyond. 'Funds for this mission outreach are generated primarily through the sale of rice and firewood donated by the believers. Every time a Mizo woman cooks rice, she places a handful in a special "missionary bowl". This rice is then taken to the local church where it is collected and sold at the market.' Visitors to the region testify to the laughing eyes and smiling faces of the people, full of warmth and joy.

Almolonga, Guatemala

The Guatemalan town of Almolonga, in the mid-1970s, was typical of many Mayan highland communities; that is, idolatrous, alcohol abusing and economically depressed. Mired in poverty and fear, solace was sought through alcohol and a local deity called Maximon. But the power of prayer changed all that. A group of local intercessors were determined to fight back and started evening prayer vigils. And the town changed dramatically. There used to be thirty-four bars for this population of 20,000. Most have been closed, as have the town's four jails, as the crime rate has declined steadily. The population has become more prosperous and orderly than its neighbours.

Almolonga is also famous for its fertile soil and abundant, king-sized vegetables. There is some controversy as to whether the vegetables owe their size to divine intervention, fertile soil or pesticides. Most likely a combination of all three. However, what is certainly owing to the gospel is the change from dissolute to responsible behaviour by the populace, which has led to a dramatic increase in their prosperity.

The Umuofia of Nigeria

The Umuofia is a people group who were steeped in the ancestral traditions of sorcery, divination and spirit appeasement. In 1996, two Christian brothers became increasingly disturbed by the spiritual state of their people. They sought to understand through fasting and spiritual discernment how the people had become so ensnared. Over time, they studied the roots and then presented their findings to a public meeting - at which the Holy Spirit fell. They encouraged the people to renounce the covenants they had made with idols and get rid of the shrines to ancestral spirits. Mass repentance ensued and many idols were publicly burned.

According to the 2014 article, almost everybody attends church meetings, and the atmosphere is very different. Things have also begun to change politically and economically. There is evidence that God has touched the land here; shortly after the public repentance, several of the villagers discovered that their plots contained saleable minerals.

Kiambu, Kenya

Located 14 kilometres north of Nairobi, Kiambu was a place of 'profligate alcohol abuse, untamed violence and grinding poverty', according to the article in *Renewal Journal*. In the late 1980s, a small group of intercessors called on the Spirit of the Lord from the basement of a grocery store, which became known as the Kiambu Prayer Cave. After believers won a spiritual battle with a local witch, the atmosphere started to change. People used to be afraid to venture out after dark, but now they enjoy one of the lowest crime rates in Kenya. The economy is growing and buildings projects abound.

Vitoria da Conquista, Brazil

A powerful move of God began in the mid-1990s in Vitoria da Conquista, a city in Brazil's Bahia state, where the population struggled under extreme poverty, corruption and violence. Spiritual renewal has since brought unity and growth to the churches, crime figures have dropped dramatically, and record coffee export figures have boosted the economy.

There are many other examples of transformed communities which are now prospering. Among them is Cali in Colombia, infamous as one of the drugs capitals of South America. Dramatic changes have taken place in this city of two million as the churches have come together to pray. The Hemet Valley in southern California is another work in progress; this centre of drug manufacture and cult activity is being transformed by the prayers of local pastors. The article also reports that 'transforming revival is also now spreading through large numbers of villages and communities in the South Pacific'.

God is at work globally. Farming God's Way (listed in the Additional Resources section) is an organization working in around twenty countries in Africa. Subsistence farmers are taught how to care for and conserve their soil using a combination of biblical guidance, good management and modern technology. The results are spectacular. Poor soil is improved, and yields are increased three to five times on average. That difference is enough to lift a family out of poverty.

God responds as his people call on him, both individually and collectively. Poor and depressed families, towns and even cities are lifted out of the 'miry pit' of hopelessness and poverty by the application of the gospel. Where there is revival, there is abundance. Many churches and mission organisations are working throughout the world, not just to bring relief but to change mindsets; from a reliance on aid to being empowered to prosper. An abundant life is not just for western Christians, it is not just the American dream dressed up as religion. While abundance may look different in different circumstances, it is within the grasp of every believer wherever they live.

By now you may well be asking what all of this means to you? What it means is that blessing us is part of God's plan. We are not alone as we take on the world. He is on our side. He gives us the power to gain wealth and be a blessing to others. Our blessings are not just for our personal benefit. They are to be shared and used to help others and further the kingdom of God. Our blessings combine to raise the level of collective blessing, increase expectation for revival and the transformation of society.

God also gives plenty of warnings about letting the desire for money become uppermost in our lives. It is a sad fact that the richer we become, the more self-centred we can be, unless we consciously decide to put God first. 'But seek first his kingdom and his righteousness, and all these things will be given to you as well.'[45] When Jesus says 'all these things', he is referring to food, clothing and the necessities of life.

In the days when I used to recruit financial advisers, I would always ask, as part of the interview process, what their goals in life were. I was almost always given the reply, 'I want to have a good life, a nice house and be successful and make lots of money'. Rarely can I remember anyone with a greater vision. I longed to hear someone say that they wanted to make the world a better place or make money so they could help orphans in Africa. Perhaps they were just telling me what they thought I wanted to hear. We need to lift our eyes from the everyday and look to a spiritual and 'other' focused vision for life. If we are seeking first his kingdom, then God will provide all we need.

If you are struggling financially, perhaps it doesn't feel as if God is on your side? Maybe it feels like he has forgotten you or he is too busy with more important things to personally intervene in your situation? There may be a number of reasons why it seems that way. Everyone's financial situation is different but if you feel you are struggling, have a look at the five reasons listed in the following chapters and see if any of them resonate with you.

PART TWO: THE PROBLEMS

Chapter 6
What Do You Really Believe?

Let me preface this second part by saying clearly that God is not like a vending machine. With a vending machine you know that if you put in the right amount of money you will get the chocolate bar or soft drink of your choice. God is not mechanistic and will not be manipulated. We cannot reduce relationship with Father God to a religious formula that achieves the right result.

Reflect on these next five chapters, in which I examine the five most common reasons I have come across where Christians struggle with money. See if any (or all!) apply to you. Then spend time in prayer asking God what actions you should take.

Reason 1: Lack of expectation

The starting place to discover what is affecting your abundance is in your head. If we do not imagine that we will witness the goodness and blessing of our Heavenly Father in our everyday lives, that will lead to wrong thinking, which leads to wrong expectations, which in turn lead to wrong actions. You've probably heard the expression 'a poverty spirit' used to describe people who seem to be concerned about every penny they spend and fear that they will run out of money. But poverty is not really a spirit. If it were then it could just be repented of and cast out. Unfortunately, it is often much more deeply embedded, an attitude of mind that is so ingrained that it colours our every action.

A poverty spirit can be changed. The problem starts with wrong thinking. Let me give you an example: A young woman in our church recently went on a date with a man from a similar evangelical background. As the evening progressed, they talked about attitudes to money. She discovered that he came from the 'godliness equals poverty' school of thought, no doubt passed down from parents. Much discussion ensued. He thought it was wrong for Christians to be prosperous and that pastors should not live in nice houses or drive good cars, because Jesus loved poor people. This was like a red rag to a bull, as she had grown up a pastor's kid and remembered how guilty they were made to feel every time they spent any money on holidays or enjoyment. Needless to say, there was no second date! If you do not believe that God wants to bless you and you do not feel free to enjoy the abundance that God has for us, then it is most unlikely that you will experience this blessing.

Let me remind you of that first sermon from Jesus, quoting from the beginning of Isaiah 61:

The Spirit of the Sovereign Lord is upon me, because the Lord has anointed me to proclaim good news to the poor. He has sent me to bind up the broken-hearted, to proclaim freedom for the captives and release from darkness for the prisoners, to proclaim the year of the Lord's favour and the day of vengeance of our God.

Jesus begins by declaring that he has come to bring good news to those who are poor. This sermon is about Jesus bringing in the kingdom and is not primarily about wealth. However, there must be a reason why Jesus (and Isaiah) speaks first to poor people. What sort of news would be good for these people? Surely that poverty was going to be less of a problem. It can't just mean that they will continue to be poor until they die but will be rich in heaven. Jesus gives them the opportunity to escape from poverty because he brings redemption and freedom.

Negative thinking

We read in Proverbs that 'as he thinks in his heart, so *is* he'.[46] Our outward circumstances are largely a product of our thoughts, feelings and choices. We attract to ourselves the things we think about and dwell upon, which can be positive or negative. Paul, writing to the Philippians, encouraged them: 'Finally, brothers and sisters, whatever is true, whatever is noble, whatever is right, whatever is pure, whatever is lovely, whatever is admirable - if anything is excellent or praiseworthy - think about such things.'[47]

Through thinking negatively, we can sabotage not only our financial wellbeing but our mental and physical health. Do you really believe that God wants you to prosper and live an abundant life? I mean really, *really* believe it? Or do you think that you should have just enough to survive, and you feel guilty if you spend any money on yourself or offended when you see what you consider to be extravagance in others?

A good test of your outlook on financial blessing is to ask yourself how you would feel if you had to set your pastor's salary. Would you treat them well? Would your guiding principle be: 'The elders who direct the affairs of the church well are worthy of double honour'?[48] Or would you tend to think that they ought to earn less than you do? What if you had the power to choose your pastor's car? Would they be driving a shiny new one or a beaten-up old banger?

Do you really believe that God wants you to have a life free from lack? Your first reaction may be to say, 'Of course I do' - but just think for a moment. Do any of these phrases come out of your mouth when financial or other setbacks occur?

'It always happens to me.'
'If things can go wrong, they will.'
'Just my luck.'
'I'll never have any money.'
'I can't do it, I'm not smart enough.'
'I just can't save money.'

Matthew writes in his Gospel: 'out of the abundance of the heart the mouth speaks'.[49] And we read in Proverbs 18 verse 21 that 'Life and death are in the power of the tongue'. Speaking negatively over ourselves will reinforce our negative and damaging beliefs, which in turn will sabotage our prosperity.

Negative beliefs damage much more than just our wealth. They can destroy relationships. In a previous church, I had a friend who was convinced that that she was constantly rejected by the other women in the church. Because she believed that, she behaved as though she had already been rejected and therefore was not a very good friend to others; hence others felt that she was rejecting them. And so the cycle continued. What you believe in the deepest part of you will manifest in outward circumstances. An apple tree will only produce apples. It will never grow oranges. It can't change its essence. Humans are different; we can change our thinking, which will change our circumstances. Our basic attitudes are usually a product of our upbringing or have been absorbed from those around us, particularly insidiously if you are working in a negative environment.

Think again about your parents' attitudes to money as you were growing up. Did they expect to gradually accumulate wealth through hard work and thrift? Were they kind and generous to others; or did they expect only trouble and poverty in this life, feeling the need to hang on to every penny? Look at your own attitudes and compare them to how your parents thought about and managed their finances. I can remember my own father's belief that making a living was a very difficult thing. As an immigrant in the UK, his father hoped to leave persecution and antisemitic discrimination behind, and he was used to hardship. It was almost as if my father expected life to be as tough for him as it had been for his father. I had in turn absorbed these attitudes and it's taken me many years to replace them with an expectation of abundance and blessing.

Familial spirits

If you look back at your family line and notice a catalogue of hardship and financial pressure, which seems impossible to escape from, then this could be a consequence of continued inherited negative attitudes. And those attitudes may have opened the way for either familial spirits or generational curses. Familial spirits are demonic entities that have lived with particular families for so long that they just seem to be part of them. It's difficult to separate the thoughts of the family members from the spirit's thoughts. They go from generation to generation through the family or bloodline. They can affect every aspect of their wellbeing, including their financial situation.

Ephesians reminds us that 'our struggle is not against flesh and blood, but against the rulers, against the authorities, against the powers of this dark world and against the spiritual forces of evil in the heavenly realms'.[50] You do not need to tolerate it any longer, if you are in a church which understands spiritual authority then do ask for help and pray with someone experienced in this sort of prayer.

If that route is not available then you can do it yourself. You can break off that spirit by asking Jesus whether you have been listening to a familial spirit, and whether it has been affecting the way you think about yourself.

Is there anyone you need to forgive? Perhaps parents or grandparents for passing down this trait. Ask Jesus for forgiveness for partnering with this spirit. Then renounce it through the blood of Jesus, thank him for breaking its power off you and declare that you will no longer hear its voice as truth. Ask Jesus to fill you afresh with his Holy Spirit.

Word curses

Sometimes harsh words or curses spoken over us can cause a deep wound that affects the way we think about ourselves and live our daily lives. I have already quoted Proverbs 18 verse 21, that life and death are in the power of the tongue. It becomes a reality when we think about the effects of pronouncements made over us by parents or teachers, which can bless or blight our whole lives.

'You'll never amount to anything.'
'You're a waste of space.'
'You're just stupid/hopeless/useless/dumb/ugly.'
'You were a mistake.'

Declarations such as these can have long-term consequences.

Through the power of the cross we can break the curse. Hand those words to Jesus and ask him to replace them with truth. Speak out that you are no longer defined by those words, repent for any way you have partnered with them, and ask him to refill you with his truth. At the back of the book I have listed some resources that I believe you will find helpful.

Negative thinking is all around us. It acts as a drain on everything. How many of us, when greeted by a friend with the usual, 'Hello, how are you?' will reply, 'Not too bad'. It may be a particularly British response, but what does it mean? Does it mean that I am just a little bad or I am not quite bad enough, or that I am just about alright? A dear friend of mine always responds with, 'I am fearfully and wonderfully made'.[51] It may be a little over the top for some, but I trust you follow his drift.

Every interaction we have with someone is an opportunity to build up, encourage and bless them, or the reverse. Every word that comes out of our mouths has power, be it positive or negative. So always speaking positively to others will gradually change our own internal thought processes. As we seek to encourage others so we will build ourselves up and increase our expectancy of blessing. One of the keys to blessing is to remember our identity as sons and daughters of the living God. We have been adopted into a royal family. We are not commoners anymore but 'kings and priests'.[52] We are children of the King and heirs to the kingdom. He will meet all our 'needs according to the riches of his glory in Christ Jesus'.[53] 'He who supplies seed for the sower and bread for food will also supply and increase your store of seed and will enlarge the harvest of your righteousness. You will be enriched in every way so that you can be generous on every occasion.'[54]

If we keep thinking of ourselves as miserable sinners saved by grace who deserve nothing but to sneak into heaven when we die, we have missed the earthly blessings of adoption which are our inheritance as kids of the King. Jesus said 'love your neighbour as yourself'[55] but many of us do not love, or even like, ourselves. Self-hatred seems to be much more common than self-love these days, with the negative bias of social media continually showing us how beautiful others are and what exciting lives they appear to be leading. As we compare ourselves, we can easily start to feel inadequate and unlovable and then be caught in a downward spiral of gloom as we sense we are somehow missing out on life. We can lose sight of who we really are.

The Bible tells us that each and every one of us is special: 'But you are a chosen people, a royal priesthood, a holy nation, God's special possession'. You are a unique creation. Jesus has chosen you to be part of his family. He will provide for you in his way and we are to live lives that please him not the world.

You can change

Everything we do, every action we take, starts off as a thought. Whatever our thinking patterns are, positive or negative, they will reflect in our actions. So, to change our actions we have to change our thoughts. According Dr Caroline Leaf, the eminent neurologist, the human mind is the most powerful thing in the universe after God. She has written extensively on how our thinking affects us and the world around us, and argues that it is possible to change the way we think.

Romans 12 verse 2 says, 'Do not conform to the pattern of this world, but be transformed by the renewing of your mind. Then you will be able to test and approve what God's will is - his good, pleasing and perfect will.' We can change and renew our minds by spending time in the word and prayer, and by consciously catching ourselves when something negative comes into our thoughts, before it comes out of our mouth. Let the reality of God's love permeate your consciousness. Recognise that he is for you not against you. He has great plans for you: 'For I know the plans I have for you,' declares the Lord, 'plans to prosper you and not to harm you, plans to give you hope and a future.' This was a promise for the Israelites in exile in Babylon, but it is one which we can claim as individuals today, as we too are his chosen people.

If you are aware of negative thought patterns running through your mind which result in negative attitudes, then start to speak out the positives. Try and catch yourself as you speak, and change your words. Ask your family or friends to help by pointing out whenever you make a negative comment. Speaking out truth will change us more quickly and effectively than just thinking it. Even God chose to speak in order to create light and life; he didn't just think the world into being. Words are like seeds which, once planted, grow into what they are describing. So, plant words of life into your life. Plant them into the lives of those you meet each day. Plant them into your family, your friends, your business and your workplace. Here are some examples of declarations to speak over yourself:

'I can do all things through Christ who strengthens me' (Phil. 4:13, NKJV).
'God has great plans for me.'
'I am God's favourite.'
'God richly supplies all my needs.'
'God's plans are to prosper me and not to harm me.'
'I will be blessed when I come in and blessed when I go out.'
'The Lord will bless everything I put my hand to.'
'The Lord will grant me abundant prosperity.'
'The Lord will make me the head and not the tail.'
'The Lord gives me the ability to produce wealth.'

Regularly speaking out these affirmations will start to transform our negative mindsets. If negative thinking is an area that needs attention in your life, I recommend two resources (listed in the Additional Resources section at the end of the book): Steve and Wendy Backlund's online materials aimed at helping the Church grow in hope, joy and renewal of our minds through Igniting Hope

Ministries; and Dr Caroline Leaf's work on detoxing and growing our brains. You may feel that your circumstances are hopeless but, to quote Steve Backlund, 'there are no hopeless circumstances, only hope challenged people'.

The first steps to enjoying the abundant life are: to agree that it is your birthright, decide that you want to prosper and experience this abundance of God, and believe that he is eager for you to step into the blessings he has for you. Then examine your thinking, catch your negative thoughts and resolve to eliminate them. Finally, speak out positive affirmations daily.

Chapter 7
Joyful Giving

Reason 2: Are you not giving joyfully?

One of the foundations for living abundantly is joyful giving; primarily, giving to God out of gratitude and also giving to those in need. It is worth, first, exploring the principle of giving from our 'first fruits' in thankfulness to God, deriving from almost the beginning of humankind. In Genesis, we see that Abel's sacrifice was acceptable to God whereas Cain's was not. Abel brought the firstborn of his flock whereas it seems Cain just brought a few vegetables. It seems that Cain's offering was much more casual than Abel's intentional giving of the best of his flock: 'But Abel also brought an offering- fat portions from some of the firstborn of his flock'.[56] In Exodus, God commands: 'Bring the best of the firstfruits of your soil to the house of the Lord your God' (Exod. 23:19; and see Lev. 2:11-16). So, the principle of giving the first fruits starts early and is then codified under the Law. Offering the first fruits is a response of gratitude to God who makes the soil fertile and causes the crops to grow. There are vestiges of the practice today in the Harvest Festival.

In the New Testament, giving is encouraged by what has been called the law of sowing and reaping: 'Remember this: whoever sows sparingly will also reap sparingly, and whoever sows generously will also reap generously'.[57] Many of us are aware that the kingdom of God works in an opposite way to that of the human race. With God, the result of giving is receiving. We do not give in order to receive but it happens as a by-product of giving. Luke writes of an abundant response that will come to those who give. 'Give, and it will be given to you. A good measure, pressed down, shaken together and running over, will be poured into your lap. For with the measure you use, it will be measured to you.'[58]

The Old Testament also introduces the practice of tithing, which is giving one-tenth of our income to God. Many have asked me whether tithing is for today, or whether it is an old covenant idea as it is hardly mentioned in the New Testament. There are arguments for and against this practice. Let us begin with the reasons why many believe that tithing is for today.

The practice of tithing originates in Genesis, where Abraham, still named Abram, gave Melchizedek, a priest of God, one-tenth of his spoils of war (Gen. 14:20). This event is referenced in Hebrews 7. When Jacob met God at Bethel, he made this promise: 'of all that you give me I will give you a tenth' (Gen. 28:22). Because these two events occurred before the *torah* (teaching) was given to Moses at Mount Sinai, the practice is said to have originated before the Law and therefore deemed valid forever, even though the Law no longer applies under the new covenant. When Moses received the *torah* on Mount Sinai, tithing was included in the instructions. Ten per cent of all agricultural produce was to be given to support the priests and Levites, as they had no inherited lands and no other means of support.

Some Christian denominations today teach that ten per cent of your income should be given to your local church, before any other charitable donations. That follows the old covenant principle, and

I have heard this described as 'paying your rent for being on the planet'. However, there might have been three tithes under the Law of Moses. First, the 'Levitical tithe', as discussed above. Second, the 'festival tithe', which was a further ten per cent, to be spent on food at the annual feasts when the people gathered to celebrate.[59] The individuals retained ownership of this tithe and ate it at the feast. You could describe it as their annual holiday expenses. The third was the 'charity tithe', a ten per cent offering approximately every three years, which was used to support Levites, widows, orphans and foreigners.[60] This means that around 23.3% of an Israelite farmer's annual income went in tithes including the amount to be consumed at the feast! The Old Testament clearly teaches the practices of tithing and of giving to special offerings, such as to help construct the Tabernacle.[61]

When we start to look at the New Testament the picture is less clear. The only time Jesus mentions tithing is when he is admonishing the Pharisees for carefully giving a tenth of their garden herbs but failing in weightier matters of love and judgement.[62] In this scenario, however, he is addressing religious Jews about the hypocrisy of their practices, not instructing his own disciples. If tithing were to continue under the new covenant, you would have thought that when James and Paul were laying down instructions to the first Gentile believers regarding changes to their behaviour now that they were grafted into Israel, they would have said something about tithing if it were meant to be practised by them; it would have been a totally new concept for most of them. However, all that was instructed was to avoid food sacrificed to idols, from eating blood, from eating the meat of strangled animals, and from sexual immorality.[63] Not a mention of what they should do with their money.

When you look more closely at the Old Testament illustrations, things become a little uncertain. In Abraham's case, the only time he gave ten per cent to anyone was from the spoils of war. He then gave the other ninety per cent back to the original owners. There is no record of Abraham giving regularly out of his income to anyone else. In Jacob's case, the idea of offering ten per cent to God in return for blessing was a way of declaring that God was his King. But Jacob's tithe was conditional on God blessing him, it was entirely Jacob's idea and there is no suggestion that it was instituted by God.

It is important to remember that the days of the Old Testament tithe were the days before income and sales taxes. Israel was a theocracy, which means not only was there no separation between Church and State, but the Church actually was the State, and the priests were the government and judiciary. The tithe money actually went to the government. Hence, you could fairly describe the tithe in ancient Israel as equivalent to today's income tax. When the Romans arrived and conquered the Middle East, they brought their ideas of taxation. They employed or rather franchised tax collectors who could extort as much as they could from the people and pass on the required share to the Roman authorities. Hence, we have Matthew the tax collector and, famously, Zacchaeus, who were hated by the people as traitors helping to support the Roman occupation.

As we can see, there are differing views as to whether or not tithing is valid today, and a full discussion and arguments for and against are beyond the scope of this book. My view is that tithing is not mandated for new covenant believers, so we are under no 'legal' obligation to give ten per cent as we are no longer under the Law. We also know that we have Jesus as our mediator between us and the Father and so we no longer have or need Levitical priests. Most of us are also not living in the land of Israel. However, that does not negate the blessings which come from giving, which are detailed in the New Testament and discussed at the beginning of this chapter.

Any discussion of the first fruits of anyone's increase, as mandated in scripture, begs the question: why should we give any more than that? In answer, we should give because we are putting God first and because giving money helps to 'enlarge the kingdom on earth'. Surely, if the new covenant is better than the old, then we should be giving more in gratitude rather than less. We have missionaries who need to be sent, pastors who need to be paid and local churches with buildings which need to be maintained. We've already looked at Paul's instructions to Timothy: 'The elders who direct the affairs of the church well are worthy of double honour, especially those whose work is preaching and teaching. For Scripture says, "Do not muzzle an ox while it is treading out the grain."'[64] The message is, church leaders deserve to be well paid. If we do not give generously, how will this happen?

Joyful giving is something which will bring blessing, whether you believe that tithing is mandated in scripture or not. So never give it grudgingly; give it joyfully as an opportunity to bless God and you will receive his blessing in return. I have discovered in my own life that you cannot out-give God. The more you give joyfully and in faith, the more will be given back to you.

If your local church is where you are fed spiritually then that is where your primary regular giving should be sent. 'If we have sown spiritual seed among you, is it too much if we reap a material harvest from you?'[65] If you are not being fed spiritually at your local church, you need to prayerfully consider why you are there. If, for whatever reason, you are not part of a local church and do not wish to be, generosity is still a key to abundance. Pick a charity, preferably one which focuses on those who are poor or disadvantaged, and give regularly. You will be amazed at the result, if you prayerfully and joyfully give. Instead of looking upon giving as something you ought, or are instructed, to do, why not think of it as a privilege; a way in which you can honour God and receive his blessings in return. Think about it as the grace of God which allows us to give and be blessed in return. Aside from the needs of the church leaders, our giving has an important effect on us.

God does not need our money. He has plenty of everything! Joyfully giving money to him (even indirectly) reminds us of our total dependence on him. The book of Proverbs tells us, 'Honour the Lord with your wealth, with the firstfruits of all your crops; then your barns will be filled to overflowing' and, 'One person gives freely, yet gains even more; another withholds unduly, but comes to poverty'.[66]

The key practical factor about giving is that it should always be done before we spend our money on something else. This is for three reasons. First, we are following the principle of the 'first fruits' of our labour being given to God. This reminds us that all our supply has come from him. It may appear to come via our employer or government agency, but it is from God, and giving back to him first is an expression of our gratitude for his goodness to us. Second, giving helps us to be free from the love of money. It prevents us from being consumed by greed and releases us from the fear of not having enough by increasing our faith, as we see how God blesses us as a result. Third, if we wait until the end of the month to see what we have left to give, it is highly likely to be little or nothing. Giving from our overdraft or on credit is not a good idea!

Giving is the one practice in the Bible where we are told to test God:

'Will a mere mortal rob God? Yet you rob me. But you ask, "How are we robbing you?" In tithes and offerings. You are under a curse - your whole nation - because you are robbing me. Bring the whole tithe into the storehouse, that there may be food in my house. Test me in this,' says the Lord Almighty, 'and see if I will not throw open the floodgates of heaven and pour out so much blessing that there will not be room enough to store it.'[67]

While that statement applied to those living under the old covenant and should not apply after the cross, as Jesus redeemed us from the curse, nevertheless the principle is the key. Put God first and cheerfully give a regular amount of your income, and test him to bless you.

There are millions of testimonies of how the Lord has blessed those who have given. Ask anyone you know who gives regularly what the effect has been. I love watching *The 700 Club* on CBN, as every day they will have another example of how giving has changed the lives of both those receiving and those giving.

How should I give joyfully?

If you are paid monthly, set up a standing order to go out on the day you are paid. I do know people who write a cheque at the beginning of every month because they want to give consciously rather than automatically. While I admire the sentiment of making conscious gifts, I know that sometimes I would forget to do it and so I stick to a standing order. If you are paid in cash, then put aside the amount you wish to give as you are paid. Put the money in a separate 'giving' account, or jar, so you can't spend it accidentally. If you wait to see what you have left over at the end of the month then it probably won't happen. The key here is to give to God first. Don't give God your leftovers; he wants to be first. If you are struggling with money and don't feel that you can give ten per cent, I urge you to test God's generosity by giving a small amount on payday and asking God to make the rest of your money stretch further. God won't let you down.

People sometimes ask whether the tithe should be net or gross (that's asking whether to give a percentage of your income before tax has been taken, or after). This is the wrong question. It's a question asked by those who feel that tithing is an obligation, not a delight. I have never had that question asked by someone who wanted to give more! My view is that it should be as much as you can give joyfully. After all, if the new covenant is better than the old then should we not want to give more rather than less? If your faith and income allow you to give twenty-five per cent or more, then great; if your faith is such that two per cent feels like a stretch then start there, and ask God to prosper you so you can increase your giving.

'Each of you should give what you have decided in your heart to give, not reluctantly or under compulsion, for God loves a cheerful giver.'[68] God does not delight in gifts given under compulsion. He wants us to give cheerfully and without any sense that this is something we have to do. God said to Moses, 'Tell the Israelites to bring me an offering. You are to receive the offering for me from everyone whose heart prompts them to give.'[69] This offering was to construct the Tabernacle so that there would be a dwelling place for God in their midst. The offerings were to be of gold, silver, bronze, coloured yarn, fine linen and hides, among others; all expensive and valuable items. What a privilege to be able to bless God with our offerings. The important points are: to give first, before we spend any money on ourselves, to give it joyfully, and to thank God for the blessing we are going to receive.

'Offerings' is the word used in scripture for giving above and beyond the tithe. The term is also used for various sacrifices for the forgiveness of sins. Those offerings are no longer needed, as Jesus became the ultimate offering for the forgiveness of our sins. Free-will offerings should be given to whoever we believe that God is prompting us to give, particularly to those in great need.

Giving to poor people is very much encouraged in scripture. The book of Proverbs has a lot to say about giving; the following verses show how blessing follows giving: 'A generous person will prosper; whoever refreshes others will be refreshed' (11:25); 'But the righteous give without sparing' (21:26); 'The generous will themselves be blessed, for they share their food with the poor' (22:9); 'Those who give to the poor will lack nothing, but those who close their eyes to them receive many curses' (28:27).

Our local church embarked on a Tsunami of Love campaign. The idea was that we were all to be especially kind and generous in day-to-day situations, as we felt led by God. Here is the story of my friend Matt:

After weeks of praying I felt God wanted me to bless cleaners who do a vital and often overlooked job. After trying to pluck up courage on numerous occasions, I was in London with work colleagues sitting on a pub balcony at Victoria Station. God drew my eyes to a cleaner working in the main area of the station and I felt I was being told to go and bless him. After a while of trying to ignore God's wishes, I finally left my colleagues and went down and gave him a £5 note. He smiled and thanked me. I went back to my colleagues and, within 30 seconds, a colleague handed me a £5 note that she said I had put in a collection some months ago, but had not been used. We moved on to another station and again I felt God draw me to a cleaner, so I went up to her and gave her a £5 note. That night as I was walking through London, I found a £5 note on the ground. I felt God telling me to bless a young family who lived near me. I decided they needed a day out and bought them some vouchers for the zoo, and put them anonymously through their letter box. A week later I unexpectedly received a 'high street' voucher for £50 from my internet provider. I will keep looking for those the Lord wants me to bless.

Generosity will make an enormous difference to your life, not only by you being blessed financially, but in many aspects of your life. Year after year, more and more studies are highlighting the benefits of generosity on both our physical and mental health. Generosity is about more than just giving money. It is an attitude of heart which includes helping others in need and volunteering with charities. Research backs the following four benefits of generosity.

Generosity makes you healthier

One study[70] found that generosity reduced high blood pressure as much as medicine or exercise. Another study, quoted in the *Handbook of Health and Social Relationships,*[71] found that participants who gave social support to people within their network had lower overall blood pressure and arterial pressure than those who did not.

Generosity will make you happier

The feel-good chemicals of endorphin, dopamine and oxytocin are triggered by giving. Doing good helps you feel good. In a study published in the journal *Science* in 2008,[72] researchers used brain-imaging technology to look at the pleasure-related centres in the brain, as individuals voluntarily donated $100 to the local food bank. The same effect was shown on the giver as the recipient.

Generosity lowers stress

After testing people with heart monitors, researchers found that if people felt they were giving too little, or being stingy, then their stress levels rose, shown by higher levels of cortisol, according to a study by Queensland University.[73] Conversely, stress reduced with generosity. Another study showed that people who did not help others had a thirty per cent higher risk of dying if they experienced a stressful life event.[74]

Generosity improves our relationships

In a study of generosity and its effect on the marriage relationship, the National Marriage Project[75] researchers found that the recipient of generosity expressed high levels of marital satisfaction.

Most importantly, generosity makes us more like Jesus. He gave himself that we might have abundant life. The more we give of ourselves and our money, the more we are transformed into his likeness. Generosity is not just about giving money, it's about a whole attitude to life, about living our lives with open hands and being kind to people. Every interaction that we have with someone carries the opportunity to leave them feeling valued.

We are blessed to have a lovely park within walking distance of where we live and most days we walk in it. There is a council employee who picks up litter and keeps the park looking pristine. My wife decided that we ought to bless this woman, and so the next time we saw her we thanked her for the job she was doing and gave her a small gift. She was moved to tears and said this the first time in nineteen years of doing that job that anyone had ever thanked her!

One of the most notable biblical examples of generosity (apart from Jesus) is Ruth. We read in the book of Ruth that she refused to leave her mother-in-law, Naomi, and go back to her own people, the Moabites, after the death of her husband. Instead, she was determined to look after Naomi and chose to travel with her back to Naomi's homeland of Israel, where Ruth was considered a stranger and an alien, from a people who were traditionally enemies of the Israelites. She went out to work in the fields so she could support herself and her mother-in-law. Here we see generosity in action, as Ruth gave of her energy and time. The result of this unselfishness was that she married a wealthy man and became part of the family line of King David.

Choose to make a difference to the way you interact with people today. Particularly those who serve you in any capacity, such as store assistants, garage attendants or bus conductors, look them in the eye, smile and help them realise that they are valued. They are not just servants at your beck and call, but each one is loved by the Creator. Let's not think of giving as an imposition but rather an opportunity to bless and be blessed; not something we have to do, but something we get to do.

Chapter 8
Seek First the Kingdom

Reason 3: Is God first in your life?

What are the priorities in your life? Does concern over money, or the lack of it, weigh heavily upon you? Is your work more important than it should be? Are you making an idol out of your family, career, dog, hobby, car? Matthew 6 verses 31-33 quote Jesus as saying: 'So do not worry, saying, "What shall we eat?" or "What shall we drink?" or "What shall we wear?" For the pagans run after all these things, and your heavenly Father knows that you need them. But seek first his kingdom and his righteousness, and all these things will be given to you as well.'

God uses prosperity, or a lack of it, to highlight where our priorities lie. If you are not clear what your priorities are then just have a look at how you spend your time and money each week. That will clearly demonstrate what you consider to be important. It is easy to think that we put God first, but what does that look like in our day-to-day activity. How much time do we actually focus on him?

God will withhold blessing in our lives if we are wandering off and putting other things before him. Deuteronomy 8 records one of a number of warnings that God gives to the Israelites concerning the need to follow his commandments:

Be careful to follow every command I am giving you today, so that you may live and increase and may enter and possess the land that the Lord promised on oath to your ancestors. Remember how the Lord your God led you all the way in the desert these forty years, to humble and test you in order to know what was in your heart, whether or not you would keep his commands. He humbled you, causing you to hunger and then feeding you with manna, which neither you nor your ancestors had known, to teach you that man does not live on bread alone but on every word that comes from the mouth of the Lord. Your clothes did not wear out and your feet did not swell during these forty years. Know then in your heart that as a man disciplines his son, so the Lord your God disciplines you. (Deuteronomy 8:1-5)

Time and time again the Israelites wandered off and served other gods. The result was always God's discipline; either through famine, as the rain did not fall, or oppression from foreign armies: both of which led to poverty. Every time the people turned back to God he redeemed and rescued them. Putting provision above the provider will always lead to problems.

Another aspect of seeking first the kingdom concerns our obedience. The first chapter of James reminds us to be doers of the word and not just hearers. Those patriarchs of the Old Testament were blessed because they obeyed God. Just imagine what would have happened if Noah had not obeyed God's instruction to build a very large boat in the middle of the desert! Joshua, as he was about to lead the people into the Promised Land, was told, 'Keep this Book of the Law always on your lips; meditate on it day and night, so that you may be careful to do everything written in it. Then you will be prosperous and successful.'[76]

As we've seen, Deuteronomy 28 lists all the blessings that would come on the Israelites if they fully obeyed God and carefully followed his commands. Just look at this list:

You will be blessed in the city and blessed in the country.
The fruit of your womb will be blessed, and the crops of your land and the young of your livestock - the calves of your herds and the lambs of your flocks.
Your basket and your kneading trough will be blessed.
You will be blessed when you come in and blessed when you go out.
The Lord will grant that the enemies who rise up against you will be defeated before you. They will come at you from one direction but flee from you in seven.
The Lord will send a blessing on your barns and on everything you put your hand to.
The Lord your God will bless you in the land he is giving you.
(Deuteronomy 28:3-8)

What would have happened if Peter had not obeyed Jesus[77] when he told him to go back out to sea and put down his nets again after a hard night's fishing with nothing to show for it? He would not only have missed his best catch ever but would probably not have become the 'fisher of men', which was his true destiny.

What about you? Are you putting other things ahead of God? Are you really seeking first his kingdom? Or are you so engrossed in work or pleasure that he has slipped down your priority list? Overemphasis on work can be driven by a desire for material things or a fear of unemployment. 'For the love of money is a root of all kinds of evil.'[78] A responsible desire to give our family the good things in life can almost seamlessly slip into a love of money. Ask yourself if your job/

business/employment is where your security lies. Jesus said that you cannot serve God and mammon (money). If your work is more important than your faith, beware! God has a way of organising your circumstances to draw your attention back to him.

I remember being made redundant from a well-paid job in a large insurance company where I had really enjoyed working for almost ten years. I had travelled many miles in that role, successfully looking after sales managers and helping to recruit financial advisers. I had left home early and returned late, enjoyed the company car and the expense account. I was proud that I had helped this company to grow its new division from a standing start to over one thousand advisers. However, markets and the economy changed so that the company then decided that this business channel was not profitable enough, streamlined, then finally disbanded all that I had worked for, as well as making my job disappear. The initial shock and feeling of rejection really hurt. I know one is not meant to take these things personally, but there is a feeling almost of bereavement when you've been 'let go'. Very clearly, when I was able to take time to reflect on what had happened, I felt that God was saying to me, 'Be careful what you give your life to, hold lightly on to things which bring you humanity's acclamation and are merely temporal. Remember who is the source of your prosperity. "But seek *first* his kingdom and his righteousness, and all these things will be given to you as well"' (italics added).[79]

Where does God fit into your schedule? Are you putting him first or do you forget him when you are not in church and the busyness of life takes over? Have you felt God calling you to a new direction in life but are too cautious or scared to follow his leading? God always provides necessary finance for paths to which he calls us.

Tony and Claire are friends of mine who felt that God was calling them to serve a church in South Africa, some years ago. Once they were there, Tony was finding it difficult to get work in his trade as a painter and decorator. In his own words:

One Sunday, we were down on the drinks rota for church but had no money to buy the milk. During the meeting a word was brought about giving financially as an act of worship and a sense that there were people in the congregation who were in need. That was us! It was very humbling as people gave to us so generously. After church a man took me aside and wrote a cheque to cover our month's rent and the children's school fees. We were then invited out for lunch and, in the afternoon, a box of groceries arrived that even included smoked salmon. A week later, someone filled our car with vegetables.

God brought this couple to a place of humility and dependence upon him as they put him first. His blessing is not just about money, it's also about changing us into his likeness. He is Jehovah Jireh, our provider.

Your financial challenges could be the result of following the world's way rather than God's. Putting God first opens us up to hear from him more often. It gives us the opportunity to receive his ideas and strategies for financial success, which are likely to be rather better than ours!

My friend Phil had been feeling like God was leading him in a new direction. He had worked for over twenty years with difficult and violent children, and his job as a deputy head of a special school was well paid. At a church meeting, he was given a prophesy that he would have three different sources of income. To cut a long story short, today Phil is working part-time for the Church, training people to handle challenging children, and running a tree-cutting business. He says that, on paper, he is earning much less than before, but God somehow makes it all work!

Spend time with your Heavenly Father each day and ask him for what you need. Then expect him to answer: it may be by words, impressions or pictures; or it may be through a change in your circumstances. Be assured, if you put him first he will guide you.

Chapter 9
Character and Integrity

Reason 4: Are you always acting with financial integrity?

Being completely upright and transparent in all your financial dealings is a prerequisite for blessing. God is very gracious, and sometimes he continues to bless people who are definitely not acting in godly ways, and at other times he allows the law of sowing and reaping to come into effect. This means that financial practices which seek to gain more by cheating or lying produce the opposite effect and make you poorer rather than richer. For example, if you are not paying all the tax which should be due on your earnings, God will not cause you to prosper. Jesus said, 'give back to Caesar what is Caesar's, and to God what is God's.'[80] If you do not pay all the tax you should then, indirectly, others will have to make up your share. Titus reminds us to be obedient to rulers and authorities[81] regardless of whether or not we agree with their policies concerning how our tax money is spent.

It is also a question of honesty. We cannot conceal income from the tax officer without lying on our tax returns. Are all your business dealings fair and honest? Or are you looking for ways to extract more cash less than honestly from your customers or your employer? If you are currently unemployed, only the state benefits you are due should be claimed for. God makes it clear: 'You shall not steal, nor deal falsely, nor lie to one another'.[82] Ezekiel prophesied about the King of Tyre and how his unfair and exploitative trading would lead to his destruction.[83] Proverbs 13 verse 11 states: 'Dishonest money dwindles away, but whoever gathers money little by little makes it grow'.

Take a few moments to search your conscience, and if there is anything niggling then take time to repent. Repentance means to change the way we think and act. Whether it's about paying your tax, or your business conduct, put it right and move on in faith. If you have stolen things, even small things from your employer for example, the enemy will build your guilt into shame. If those pens and post-it notes, or more valuable items, have somehow made their way into your home, you need to find ways of returning them or recompensing the company, so that the enemy has no hold on you. It's not worth sacrificing the favour of God for a few extra pounds. It's never too late; God is the God of second chances.

Spiritual attack

The general principle is that God will bless righteousness, but it is possible to be completely honest and deal fairly with everyone yet still have financial difficulties. We have an adversary who will seek any opportunity to cause difficulties of all kinds, including financial, in our lives. You may be under specific attack from the enemy as your Christian activity is becoming more of a threat to his territory. He will always seek to exploit any weak spots so, if you have a tendency to worry about money, the enemy will attempt to create difficulties in that area, to shift your focus from kingdom activity.

The answer is to spend time seeking God and praying for his protection and blessing. Put on the full armour of God every morning as you get dressed!

Finally, be strong in the Lord and in his mighty power. Put on the full armour of God, so you can take your stand against the devil's schemes. For our struggle is not against flesh and blood, but against the rulers, against the authorities, against the powers of this dark world and against the spiritual forces of evil in the heavenly realms. Therefore put on the full armour of God, so that when the day of evil comes, you may be able to stand your ground, and after you have done everything, to stand. Stand firm then, with the belt of truth buckled round your waist, with the breastplate of righteousness in place, and with your feet fitted with the readiness that comes from the gospel of peace. In addition to all this, take up the shield of faith, with which you can extinguish all the flaming arrows of the evil one. Take the helmet of salvation and the sword of the Spirit, which is the word of God. And pray in the Spirit on all occasions with all kinds of prayers and requests. (Ephesians 6:10-18)

Does it feel like the world is against you? Do your plans turn to dust? Does it feel as though there is a saboteur in your home? We mustn't forget that we have an adversary who wishes to negate the blessings of God and to create discord in our lives. He will take any opportunity that he can find to impact our lives. 'The thief comes only to steal and kill and destroy.'[84] Any dishonesty on our part will give him an opening into our lives. Let me make it quite clear, I am not talking about 'demon possession'. I don't believe that a Christian can be demon possessed, as we have already committed ourselves to Jesus. However, any of us can be oppressed or harassed by negative or demonic entities. We must ensure that they have no landing place which will allow them to gain a foothold. If the enemy has a foothold in our lives he will turn it into a stronghold. How does he do that? He does it by latching on to negative emotions and also sin. Financial impropriety is sin. You cannot get rid of demonic oppression while you are continuing to sin.

If you know that there is no unrighteousness in your financial dealings, you can stand on the word of God and command Satan to leave you alone. I find that declaring the following verses over myself, several times a day, really helps to unblock the flow: 'The Lord has dealt with me according to my righteousness; according to the cleanness of my hands he has rewarded me'[85] and 'Whoever pursues righteousness and love finds life, prosperity and honour'.[86]

The devil will still sometimes whisper in your ear, even if you are leading a blameless life and following God. After all, he had a go at Jesus who was sinless. Follow Jesus' example and resist: 'Resist the devil, and he will flee from you' (James 4:7). Remember that you are loved by God, and that you can never lose that love, whatever the enemy may try to tell you. Tell the devil to go away, and praise God instead of listening to lies.

Chapter 10
Hey, Big Spender

Reason 5: Are you spending more than you are earning?

'Too many people spend money they haven't earned, to buy things they don't want, to impress people they don't like' (Will Smith).

Sometimes the answer to our financial problems is not as complicated as we think. It can be that we are simply not paying attention to how much we spend. Do you know where your money is going? Spending money is much more fun than tracking it! Feeling that we must have things because our friends or neighbours have them is a quick way into debt. It's a sure sign that we are listening to the wrong voices. Advertising and marketing would not be everywhere if they didn't work. So beware, before you make that large purchase, ask yourself some questions. Do I really need it? Why do I want it? Is it because others have it? If I buy it will I still be pleased with it in a year's time? Do I think God would want me to have it? Can I afford it?

We need to keep the right perspective when thinking about money. 'Thinking about money is so boring,' is a view I have heard expressed from time to time. While I am inclined to agree, if we don't master our money, the lack of it and the concern about having enough will master us. We will be led in life by what we think we can afford rather than by the will of God.

We go through an education system - primary and secondary schools, sometimes on to university - but for what purpose? To help us understand the world we live in. So that we have some knowledge of our history and culture. So that we can read and write and add up, certainly. But the main focus of the education system is to fit us for a life in the workplace; to enable us to become gainfully employed and to meet the needs of an employer. Education gives us the ability to generate income through employment. What the education system does not teach us, however, is to understand how the money we earn works or how to look after it. The system equips us for employment, to become wage slaves. Very rarely, if ever, will it encourage creativity and ingenuity in relation to the money we expect to earn. It does not train us to take control of our own financial destinies.

The path of career progression from apprentice/trainee to senior director is one of increasing knowledge and competence, where financial reward tends to go hand in hand with that increase. For most people their increase in income is more than matched by increasing spending. I know a senior lawyer who earns close to a million pounds a year, yet says he can't afford to save! Whatever we want to do in life, whether it be following a conventional career path, or becoming an artist or entrepreneur, we need to eat and afford a roof over our heads. We are all either mastering our money or it is mastering us. Only by understanding how money flows in and out and paying some attention to it will we be able to do the things we want to in life.

Therefore, taking some time to focus on understanding and controlling your money is not only worthwhile, but vital. Even if it seems boring, you need to know how it works and how much of it you need or want. Are you finding it difficult to control your spending? It may be that just a bit more focus and planning of your resources will be enough to get you out of trouble.

If our education system hardly touches on personal spending and managing our own resources, where and how do we learn? We rely on parents, friends and the 'university of life' to set our spending priorities. These are all imperfect teachers and it's quite easy to listen to the wrong voices. The world of advertising and marketing seems to shout much louder than the quiet voice of reason within. If you do not plan your spending when your pay packet arrives, you may tend to act on impulse and buy more than you can afford. We've all done it at some point. My personal weaknesses are for cameras and computers. For others, it may be shoes or watches. For a young woman I met while training some students in South Africa, it was handbags. She was most concerned to know if she should buy a very expensive handbag and make it last for years, or buy cheap ones annually!

In the next chapter, I will discuss budgeting, which is a way of planning our expenditure. At this point, however, it is worth just looking at what we are spending our money on, as there could be some simple things that can be easily corrected. For example, convenience foods - whether that's eating out, getting takeaways or just heating up prepared meals from the supermarket - have a way of eating up our money. Leisure and entertainment always seem to cost more than we expected. A simple coffee shop stop each day can add up to a substantial sum. For those of us with children of a certain age, the pressure to buy branded clothing and the latest smartphone may be almost overwhelming.

Have a good look at what you spend your money on. Try writing down each day for a week exactly what you have spent that day, and on what. By the end of a week you may notice patterns which could point to where overspending is taking place.

How much do you want?

It's easy to answer the question, How much money do I want? with, As much as I can get! It may seem a silly question, but we need to be clear about why we need money. Otherwise we run the risk of being driven by the desire to get more to the exclusion of other goals in life. If you ask yourself, 'Do I have enough money?' the answer depends on what you want that money for. If you are able to do what you feel God has called you to at this time, it's likely that you have enough. Therefore, you are on the way to achieving your goal because you have clearly identified it.

Our financial goals will vary at different stages of life. Many young people want that nice car and smart clothes to impress. Some singles and many couples want to buy their own property. Some may well start to save for their children's education and futures. As we get older, we become aware that one day we will not be able to earn money any longer and need to have some funds to generate an income for later life. If we do not take control of our money and plan to save as well as spend, we will be unlikely to accumulate enough for a comfortable life in the future.

Perhaps you are already believing for abundance, giving generously, acting righteously and seeking first God's kingdom, but you still seem to be short of cash. There are a number of helpful steps to take in order to be really in charge of your money. In Part Three, we will explore the practicalities of being in control, beginning by making it personal.

PART THREE: THE SOLUTIONS

Chapter 11
So, What Do I Do Next?

We have explored the need to think and speak abundantly, and to ensure we are giving generously and acting righteously. Now it's time to get practical, and examine your individual balance sheet and spending habits. This is because you have to know where you are now before you can be somewhere else. Your personal balance sheet will show your net worth or net debt; what you own or what you owe.

A balance sheet is a list of your assets (what you own). Make a list of these, and their values, on the left-hand side of a sheet of paper:

Cash in the bank
Any investments (ISAs, unit trusts, shares, etc.) and pension funds
Value of any property you own
Resale value of car, bike, etc.
Resale value of valuables, jewellery, pictures, antiques, etc.

On the right-hand side, make a list of what you owe and the amounts outstanding:

Mortgage balance
Overdrafts or loan balances
Credit card debt
Student loans
Car loans

Total the two columns of amounts, and subtract the 'what you owe' column from the 'what you own' column. The difference between the two is your net worth; ideally this should be a positive figure but it may be a negative one. If so, do not be discouraged. For many young people in their first few years of a career, the effects of student debt may be substantial on their balance sheets. For those of us not recently out of further education, however, the balance sheet can be the first indication that there is a problem. There is no right or wrong amount as regards personal wealth, but it is important to know your starting point for any planning.

Clearly, older people are likely to have accumulated more assets. However, the main point of this exercise is to check that you are solvent, which means that you have enough to pay your debts. If you had died yesterday, would your legacy be a blessing to those left behind or would you be leaving your debts for them? If you find that your debts exceed your assets, it is time to take action to correct the situation.

Life assurance is a must if other people (partners, parents or children) are dependent on your income. My view is that provision should be made so that the surviving partner would have a property without needing a mortgage, and enough cash for them not to have to work until the youngest child is at school. If you have a UK student debt, it can be ignored in this calculation as they are cancelled on death and are not inherited. Paul gives instructions about the care of widows and states, 'Anyone who does not provide for their relatives, and especially for their own household, has denied the faith and is worse than an unbeliever.'[87] Life assurance protection cover is so cheap, particularly at younger ages these days, so adequate provision for your dependants should not be a stretch.

Budgeting

The balance sheet you have just created shows your 'capital account'. This is impacted by your income and expenditure, so the next step is to look at your patterns of earning and spending. This is where adjustments may need to be made.

First, I encourage you to thank God for his generosity; that he has provided for you so far and he has good things in store for you. Now, examine what money comes in and how it goes out; in other words, track your spending. This is known as budgeting and can feel pretty boring! I have tried to think of ways to make budgeting more exciting but so far have not come up with any. It is a chore, but then so is cleaning our teeth and washing up, both of which still need to be done regularly! Think of it as financial hygiene.

Proverbs tells us, 'The wise have wealth and luxury, but fools spend whatever they get'.[88] If you ignore this budgeting exercise you may well regret it. Its purpose is to make sure that you can pay for the things you have to pay for each month, such as rent, mortgage and utility bills, before spending what you have left. It's the way to stay out of debt.

Budgeting is very simple to do. Take a large sheet of lined paper and draw a line from top to bottom through the middle. On one side, list your monthly income after tax. On the other, list all your fixed and essential spending. An alternative is to use a spreadsheet or a budgeting app; there are plenty available for free. It's worth checking your bank statement to see what you are actually spending each month; this way, you can't fool yourself.

First, list all your essential spending. By essential, I mean the items that will have negative consequences if you don't pay them, for example, eviction from your property, repossession of your car, or having your gas, electricity or water cut off. And don't forget those bills which come in annually. Your list will include some of the following costs: rent/mortgage; council/property tax; electricity/gas/ water; essential transport; childcare; and insurance premiums.

Second, divide the annual total by twelve and include this figure. Add in the amounts you give in offerings and donations each month, as these are an essential key to prosperity. If you deduct your essential spending total from your after-tax income, you will have a figure for the amount available for your discretionary spending. For example: monthly income, £1,500; essential bills, £1,000; available to spend, £500. This is the money over which you have choice and control. You will have noticed that I haven't included food in the essential spending list. This is because that figure can vary so much, according to what you buy and where you buy it.

Your discretionary spending will be made up of supermarket bills, some petrol costs, eating out, entertainment, takeaways and all those coffees from Starbucks, plus those monthly small subscriptions to Apple, Spotify, Netflix, etc. When you add up your month's actual spending on these items and compare it with the 'available to spend' figure, you will be able to see whether you are living within your income or not. I have provided an example of a monthly budget sheet, for reference.

Monthly Budget

Income - After Tax	Amount
Income #1	
Income #2	
Other	
Total Income	

Essential Expenses	Amount
Giving	
Savings	
Housing - Mortgage/Rent	
Electric	
Gas	
Water	
Phone	
Cable	
Council Tax	
Transport to Work	
Internet	
Car Insurance	
Credit Card Payment #1	
Credit Card Payment #2	
Credit Card Payment #3	
Childcare	
Loan Payment	
Car Payment #1	
Car Payment #2	
Car Repairs	
Petrol	
Household (Non-Food)	
Clothes	
Haircuts	
Gifts - Birthdays and Holidays	
Social and Entertainment	
Other	
Other	
Other	
Other	
Other	
Total Expenses	
Surplus/Shortage	

Tracking spending is a particularly painful exercise for those who have a 'head in the sand' mentality towards their finances. I have known people who were so scared of money that they just piled bills in a drawer unopened, until they could not fit any more in and they had a clear out! Working with a number of people like this over the years, I have found that the 'ignore it until it cannot be ignored' approach is usually driven by fear. When forced to confront the situation, people often discover that it wasn't as bad as they had anticipated. The sense of relief and freedom which comes is worth the pain of confrontation.

Once you've finished this exercise, you will be presented with one of three scenarios:

1 You are spending less than your income each month; cash is accumulating in your account.

2 You are around the break-even mark; some months are better than others and your head is just above water, but you struggle to save anything.

3 You are spending more than your income each month; either with a growing bank overdraft and/or increasing credit card debt, as you are only making the minimum payments each month.

It is worth planning your budget, even if your financial situation relates to the first scenario. Various experts have suggested how a budget should be structured. Elizabeth Warren, the US Senator, has come up with the 50/30/20 budget, where people should try to spend no more than fifty per cent of their income on essentials (including food), thirty per cent on wants (including entertainment and holidays) and twenty per cent on savings or debt repayment. Dave Ramsey, the American personal money expert, would put the essentials figure at around sixty per cent, the wants figure at fifteen to twenty per cent, and the giving and saving at twenty per cent. There is no correct answer, as everyone is different, but if you are spending too much in one area, you are likely not to have enough to cover the others.

If you find that you have more essential bills to pay than you thought, and you are spending more than you are earning each month, then one of two things needs to happen. Either you need to find a way to reduce your monthly outgoings, which may mean a change of habits or even of housing, or you need to earn more money. It's simple; either earn more or spend less. I appreciate that simple does not necessarily mean easy. The solution is straightforward even if it may involve some discomfort. These are the only two variables in your financial situation.

If you have found that your monthly spending exceeds your income then it's likely that you will have run up some credit card debt or a bank overdraft. Both are very expensive forms of borrowing; they are another reason why this budgeting exercise is vital. A budget is for us to tell our money where to go, instead of wondering where it went. If there just doesn't seem to be enough money to live the life of abundance, you either have to increase your income or reduce your spending.

It's important to see how those monthly bills can be reduced relatively painlessly. Our largest costs usually relate to housing, the utilities associated with it, essential transportation and food. While the tips offered below may not be applicable to every circumstance, the principles apply to all of us.

First, check that you are not overpaying for anything. There are switching sites to help you reduce your costs for gas and electricity, as well as insurance, and you may be able to get a better deal by refinancing your mortgage loan, which could all save quite a lot. I have to confess to being lazy when it comes to checking that I am getting the best rates for everything.

Recently, I went through all my spending carefully, to see where I could save money. The results were very worthwhile, and I'm wondering why I didn't do it sooner: I have changed energy suppliers, and expect to save around £200 a year; house insurance is reduced by £120 a year; and boiler insurance by £160. My TV and broadband package had crept up over the years and I found I was paying for some services I didn't use and some channels I never watched; thus, I managed to trim £40 a month off the bill. A SIM-only mobile phone deal costs me £6 a month, which will be a substantial saving as long as I keep using my old phone!

Car payments can take a chunk out of our income. Sometimes it's inevitable, because we might need a car for work or family. However, it does not have to be a new car, or even a nearly new car. A five-year-old vehicle will generally work as well as one that is two years old, and be a lot cheaper to buy.

Those are the larger and largely unavoidable monthly expenditures. The next biggest tends to be food. I don't want to state the obvious but, for the sake of completeness: some supermarkets are cheaper to shop in than others! Supermarkets' own brands are less expensive than well-known branded products. Loose fruit and vegetables are usually cheaper than those that are prepackaged. Always make a shopping list and stick to it, don't be diverted. Supermarkets are laid out to entice you to spend more than you had anticipated. Have you noticed that the bread and milk are always located at the back of the store so you can be tempted by so many lovely things on the way?

Cooking from scratch is much cheaper than buying takeaways or convenience foods. Many of us lead busy lives and admit that we do not have time to cook properly. The secret is to batch cook. Whenever you cook a meal, try and cook three or four times as much as you would eat, and freeze the other portions. That way, on the days when you really don't have time to cook, you can pull a healthy meal out of the freezer rather than resort to buying expensive takeaways. Batch cooking does take a certain amount of planning but, if you plan your meals you can plan your shopping, which will reduce your costs. Beware of food shopping when you are hungry!

Are you buying your lunch out while at work? Could you take a packed lunch to save money? Do you pick up a coffee on your way in to work? Could you make one at home and transport it in a reusable cup? Even small amounts saved in these ways will add up by the end of the month. However, if your monthly shortfall is large then more drastic action is needed. Our highest expenditure almost always relates to housing; you may need to find somewhere cheaper to live, or possibly take in a lodger to share the costs.

Preparing and planning your budget is only part of the challenge. Sticking to it is the next step. One method is to use an updated version of mothers (or grandmothers) jars or envelopes, using different bank accounts. Have your salary paid into one account and then immediately transfer the amount you are going to give into another account, followed by the amount needed for your monthly essential expenses into a third account, and then the amount you are going to save or use for debt reduction into a fourth. The account your salary was originally paid into is then left as the amount of money you can spend that month on items of your choice. Use only cash or a debit card on that account for your spending.

See illustration overleaf.

Jar method for regular income.

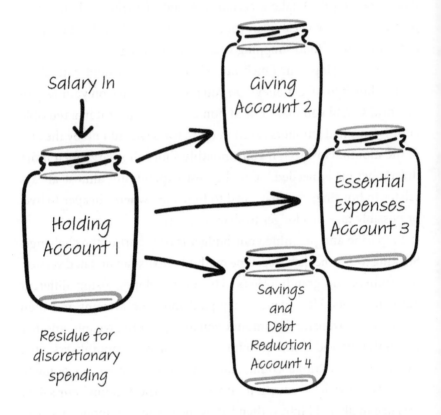

If you are self-employed, the jar system works a little differently. For many, income does not come in regular monthly payments but sporadic lumps when jobs are completed. You need to use your business account as your short-term savings account and build up some cash reserves so that you can then withdraw a steady monthly income. In addition to your other jars, you need to put aside money from every payment for income tax.

Jar method for irregular and untaxed income.

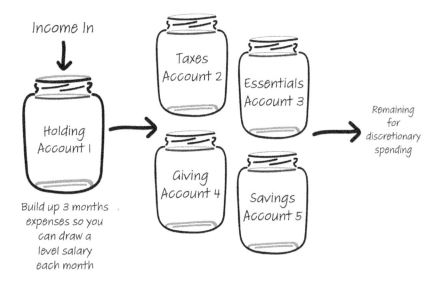

I can't overstress the importance of building up a cash reserve in your business account, as it protects you when you're unable to work for a short time, such as during illness, and enables you to pay for holidays. Easier said than done, you may say; however, if you can build that reserve it massively reduces your day-to-day stress levels.

If you are still struggling to stick to your budget then identify what is busting it. Is it overspending in the grocery store or too many meals or drinks out? Once the problem is clearly identified, you can take action. Before making big changes to your life don't forget to ask God first, and spend some time waiting on him for answers. His plan is likely to be better than yours.

Increasing our income

The alternative to micromanaging our expenditure is to increase our income, which frankly has always been my preferred route. First, I suggest you pray and make sure that you have cleared any of the potential obstacles to prosperity outlined in the earlier chapters. Then ask God, who 'gives you the ability to produce wealth',[89] what to do next. If you need to request a pay rise, ask God to give you favour with your boss and to bring about the right moment to ask. You may need to find a better paying job; ask him to show it to you. If you need more business, ask him how to obtain it. Pray for a blessing on your current customers and that they would refer new ones to you. My friend Phil, who has a tree cutting company, needed more business. He felt God telling him to be thankful for everything that he had provided, even the small, 'hardly worth doing' jobs which he had considered turning down, As he started to do that so God has massively increased his turnover, with new customers contacting him.

Perhaps you don't feel that you should be changing your employment but just need a bit more each month. Do you need an extra source of income? The way to build wealth is through having multiple sources of income. Apparently, the average millionaire has seven different streams of income. Bishop T.D. Jakes (in a YouTube sermon entitled 'Bishop TD Jakes Speaks on Multiple Streams of Income') says that Christians should have four different streams, on the basis that Adam was resourced in the garden of Eden by four different rivers. Ecclesiastes 11 begins: 'Ship your grain across the sea; after many days you may receive a return. Invest in seven ventures, yes, in eight; you do not know what disaster may come upon the land.' Diversify your sources of income and then you will not be overdependent on your job. That sounds easier said than done, but it is not as hard as we might think.

There are two different types of extra income: the 'active' and the 'passive'. The active is where you get some extra work through a part-time job or business. Depending on where you live, there are lots of part-time jobs, from care assistant to retail food sampler (which is offering samples of foodstuffs to shoppers); and there always seem to be casual food-service jobs available. If you have a particular skill, such as woodwork or repairing cars, you can put that to profitable use. Dog-walking and gardening can both provide income and give you exercise, if you enjoy the outdoors.

It has never been so easy to work from home and supplement your income with a 'side hustle'. This is passive income. All you need is a computer and internet connection. If you google 'making extra money UK' then 522,000,000 results appear; if you do the same for the US, 1,070,000,000 results pop up! You are not alone in your need for more. But beware! Not every site offering opportunities is genuine.

Beware of those sites that offer allegedly sure-fire ways of making extra money through stock market trading, spread betting, cryptocurrency (such as bitcoin) or foreign exchange trading (forex). Good money can be made, but according to one reputable trading website, Plus500, 76.4% of people who used it for spread betting, trading options or contracts for difference (which are financial instruments enabling you to speculate on financial markets) have actually lost money! You have to be prepared to research and learn about these markets before you commit any cash. I do not invest in anything I do not understand. Beware of any organisation that wants you to pay them for the privilege of working for them before you start, unless it is for purchase of stock to resell. If it is for stock, then don't buy it until you have seen it and spoken to others who have done the same and shown whatever product it is to be saleable. Multi-level marketing (Amway, Avon, etc.) can work well but you have to work quite hard to be successful. They would fall into the active rather than the passive system.

Start with your gifts and talents, as virtually anything can generate an income stream. What are your passions? What are you good at? Do you have a hobby? Whatever you can do well can be turned into an e-book, an online course, a blog or YouTube videos, and all can make money either through sales or advertising. It takes some time and energy, as books and courses need to written before they can be sold, and products need to be chosen and sourced. But once it's done then the returns just keep coming - sometimes even when you are asleep. The internet is full of free or inexpensive courses to help you learn how to start a business, a blog, YouTube channel or even on how to learn coding.

There are lots of other ways to make money through the internet. If you can make any sort of craft items, Etsy is an online marketplace to display and sell your creations. Running your own store via Amazon or eBay is not as difficult as it sounds. You hardly need any money to start as you can use a technique known as 'drop-shipping' (where items are sent direct from your supplier to your customer). Once you have decided on the sort of products you want to sell then you have to source them. There are plenty of manufacturing and wholesale companies in China, for example, who will send your product directly to your customer, so that you never need to handle the item. You then need to set up your listing on eBay at an appropriate price, and away you go. You don't have to buy any stock until you have sold it. Brilliant! Again, there are lots of websites where you can check out how to set up a drop-shipping business, who will also point you to some reliable suppliers. Once you have gained a bit of confidence in the process, you can move on to 'fulfilment by Amazon' (FBA). This is where you actually buy bulk stock, which can be as little as ten pieces, and then send them to Amazon's FBA warehouse. This way they can be listed as 'prime' and be with your customers as soon as the next day. Anybody can be an online retailer!

Do you enjoy car boot sales? You can make good money by buying at them and selling the items on eBay. Obviously, the key to success is buying stuff for less than you could sell it; eBay makes it easy for you to know what items are worth. By using the advanced search facility, eBay will show what things have sold for recently, so you will know how much or, rather, how little to pay for them to be able to resell at a profit.

If you don't want to be a shopkeeper, there are plenty of other ways to earn from the internet. Have a look at online courses and you will see the variety of skills being taught. Don't worry if someone has already done what you want to do. The global market is vast and there is room for all. There's no need to invent or discover something new, as whatever product or service seems popular always has room for another supplier. Blogs, books and courses are freely available to get you started. Pinterest is also a wonderful website for money-making ideas. The choice is yours. Spend less or earn more - or why not do both?

Mr Micawber, a character from Dickens' novel *David Copperfield*, is often quoted concerning his recipe for happiness: 'Annual income twenty pounds, annual expenditure nineteen [pounds] nineteen [shillings] and six[pence], result happiness. Annual income twenty pounds, annual expenditure twenty pounds ought and six[pence], result misery.' The truth of that definition has not wavered an inch over the years. In today's language, if your income exceeds your expenses you will be a lot happier than if your spending is greater than your income. As they say, 'it's not rocket science'.

Chapter 12
What To Do About Debt?

'Be very careful, then, how you live - not as unwise but as wise, making the most of every opportunity, because the days are evil.'[90] Debt is unwise, but it is a fact of life. There are a number of Bible verses in the book of Proverbs advising against debt and nowhere is it recommended. However, it is important to understand that debt in itself is not sin. Our eternal salvation is not lost by being in debt. I will say it again: debt is not sin.

There are many reasons why people get into debt, some of which are the result of external circumstances such as unemployment or long-term sickness. You must not think that you have fallen out of favour with God, even if you have not been careful enough with your spending. We read in 2 Kings chapter 4 that Elisha helps the widow of one of the company of prophets whose creditor was going to seize her two sons as his slaves. Even someone who hears from God and is in the company of prophets is not immune from debt. Elisha does not condemn the departed for overspending, and just wants to help the widow.

Matthew reports Jesus as saying, 'do not turn away from the one who wants to borrow from you.'[91] Jesus does not condemn borrowing but encourages us to lend to those who are in need. However, repayment will almost always be required. We read, 'Give to everyone what you owe them' (Rom. 13:7).

Good debt and bad debt

There is a school of thought that says all debt is bad, and I understand their reasoning: Proverbs 22 verse 7 says, 'the borrower is slave to the lender'. However, it is just not realistic for most of us to expect to save enough for a house or flat from our disposable income. It's hard enough to save for a decent deposit, let alone a whole property. A property mortgage is a reasonable form of debt and is usually around the lowest cost of borrowing in terms of interest paid. If you decide that all debt is wrong then you will almost certainly be paying rent to fund your landlord's mortgage all your life!

Another acceptable use of debt is to fund education, as long as that education is going to enable you to earn enough to eventually pay it off. Higher education is necessary for many occupations. Just think carefully about what you want to achieve before you commit to a three- or four-year course of study which could leave you £50,000 in debt, and still not guarantee a career with decent earnings.

Aside from these two examples, debt is to be avoided if at all possible. The other big purchase which almost everyone seems to be required to make these days is a car. While you may need a car to get to work because of the vagaries of public transport, or because you have too far to cycle, you don't need to buy a fancy one. You may want a BMW or Mercedes, but you don't actually need one. I like nice cars as much as anyone, but I have yet to sell a car for more than I paid for it. Cars, like so many other goods, depreciate in value; they are worth less each year until they do become worthless. (The one exception is the purchase and maintenance of a classic or vintage car, which should appreciate.) Nice cars are expensive, and we need to think carefully before buying one. Here are some questions to ask before committing to a purchase: Do I have to borrow to buy this car? Can I afford it? What is the interest rate being charged? How much will I be paying for it when I add in the additional interest? It's also a good idea to ask God for his opinion.

If your income is such that you can afford a really nice car then buy it and enjoy it. Just remember how much the money you have committed to spend on this beautiful vehicle is costing you in lost interest or investment growth. Beware of reasoning that just because you can afford the payments each month it must be alright to sign on the dotted line.

My definition of good debt is where the amount you borrow will purchase assets that will grow, retain their value or generate an income greater than the interest cost. Your property should retain its value in real terms and your education should enable you to earn more. Good debt would also include borrowing to buy a second property that will generate more income than you are paying in interest. You may need to borrow in order to start or expand your business. This can also be good debt. In general, I would counsel against it, if you can possibly avoid it. Businesses almost always take longer than you expect to become profitable and getting burdened with debt repayments too soon can cause problems. Once you have a successful business running, borrowing for expansion can be beneficial. Most of today's great corporations have borrowed to grow.

Bad debt is defined as money which has been borrowed to be spent on consumption or buying more stuff. It is money borrowed with nothing to show for it except perhaps our expanding wardrobe or waistline! It creeps up, as we spend more each week on eating out, clothes and entertainment than we have available. That's why the budgeting exercise is so important. The average consumer debt per household in the UK currently is around £15,400[92] excluding mortgages. This figure is likely to have grown owing to the COVID-19 pandemic. I suspect that many are reading this book because you are already in debt and are wondering (or desperate to know) how to get out of it.

Credit card debt is the most likely culprit. Credit cards are very handy things; in fact, far too handy! The plastic almost painlessly allows us to buy so many things that we think we really need - at least until the bill arrives! Wonderfully convenient, it becomes easier and easier to spend money. 'Buy now, pay later' is the mantra, but it's remarkable how soon 'later' arrives! We can just tap our card onto the reader or wave our smartphone at it and it's done. Cards are even embedded in our watches. It will not be long before we will be able to shop by facial expression!

The first step is to eliminate credit card debt. It's vital to understand that if we do not pay our credit cards off in full every month then trouble is brewing. Because their interest charges are so high, any unpaid debt at the end of the month will grow rapidly. That interest will compound and the following month we will start paying interest on the interest. The tendency is then to use our credit card more, to cover any monthly shortfalls, which will gradually make things worse. It's frighteningly easy to find that we are in a downward spiral of debt, which grows like a snowball rolling down a hill.

Albert Einstein, history's most famous scientist, is said to have described compound interest as 'the eighth wonder of the world': 'He who understands it, earns it ... he who doesn't ... pays it'. Yet it's easy to underestimate the effects of debt, reasoning that 'it's only a small amount' or 'everybody has some'. These are signs that you are in denial and not in control.

Credit cards are fine if they are managed. I am not saying every card should be cut up on sight. The challenge is to learn to use them responsibly. I know Jesus didn't carry a credit card but then he never had to hire a car or be concerned about whether his credit rating was high enough to qualify for a mortgage. If you use your credit card responsibly then you demonstrate that you can handle credit well, which greatly improves your chances of qualifying for a property mortgage. Relying on your memory to pay the monthly bill when due is very dangerous. It's so easy to forget and end up with late payment charges and a potentially blighted credit record. In my work as a mortgage adviser, I came across people whose credit score was lower than it should have been, just because they had been a few days late on two or three occasions when making their monthly payment. The best thing to do is set up a direct debit or bank mandate to pay the outstanding balance each month. The card companies don't exactly encourage us to pay off everything each month as they make their money from the interest we pay. A few months ago, I took out a new credit card because it offered me air miles on my purchases. When I tried to set up a direct debit to pay off the total balance every month, it initially only allowed me to set up to make the minimum monthly payment automatically; I had to go online at a later date to alter the payment to the total outstanding balance.

If you are in the position where your credit card debt has already built up, there are practical steps to take. First, pray. Ask God to help you with your day-to-day buying decisions, to give you strength to resist temptation and become debt-free. You will find that God amplifies the speed of your debt repayment. Every testimony I have heard where people really set themselves to pay off debt tells the same story. God seemed to intervene to speed up the whole process, and they were out of debt far quicker than they expected.

Here are the practical steps to take next.

1 Have a clear picture of where you are. Write a list of all your debts, who the lender is and how much you currently owe, along with the interest rate and minimum payments.

2 Before you start overpaying, build a small emergency fund, say £500. This is to take care of those unforeseen events that will occur. Whether it's new tyres for the car or needing a plumber, the only way to prevent further credit card spending is to have an emergency fund so that you can pay without increasing your debt.

3 If you have balances on a few different cards, then the sensible thing to do is to start overpaying the one which charges the highest interest rate. Tackle them one at a time, and focus on shifting that debt as quickly as possible by paying more than the minimum required each month. Another approach is to work on the one with the smallest outstanding balance first. As you pay this one off, your motivation to tackle the next one should increase.

4 Plan your monthly budget to include the card repayment. Decide which card to pay off first and focus all your overpayment on that one. Set it up by direct debit the day after you are usually paid, to make sure it goes out before you can spend it. If you have a spouse or partner, make sure that they are in agreement on the way forward.

5 You may be able to switch your credit card debt(s) to a different provider. Some companies are still offering reasonable interest-free periods which would reduce any growth in your debt. That way you will limit the growth of the outstanding balance.

6 Make sure you have direct debits in place to cover each card's minimum amount each month. You can make your extra payments by bank transfer or cheque, but don't risk any more of those late-payment charges.

7 Stop using your credit card. If you find some months that you cannot get by without using your card, you need to re-examine and readjust your monthly budget.

8 Alongside these steps, pray for miraculous provision. If you make the effort to reduce debt then God often blesses and multiplies the effect.

Ideally, don't use your credit card again until your debt is clear, and you know you will be able to pay for everything you are spending on the date the card payment is due. Getting out of debt is like losing weight; hard work, but the results come if you are consistent. Staying out of debt is just the same as keeping that weight off; you can't just go back to old habits!

Secret debt

A 2018 survey[93] in the UK of 4,000 people found that nearly one in three (29%) who were in a relationship said their partner did not know about all the money they owed. You could call it financial infidelity! The head of the debt advice service that carried out the survey said that people concealed debts to protect their loved ones, or because they were concerned about being judged. However, she added, 'This rarely solves the issue. In fact, it often makes things worse.'

If you are hiding debt from your partner, I urge you to pluck up the courage to talk to them about it, because it will come out sooner or later. They will open a letter or take a phone call, and it will be too late. It's so much better to find out from you, rather than the person to whom you owe money. A great deal of harm can come to your relationship if they find out this way, as your partner may feel that their trust has been betrayed. If you really feel that you cannot share it with them, either because of fear, shame or just embarrassment, then I urge you to seek help.

Debt: manageable or out of control?

There are times when we all need to buy something which costs more than the amount we can readily lay our hands on. Be it a new central heating boiler or new furniture, these products usually come with some sort of a 'buy now, pay later' offer. Though certainly worth checking out, these are not always the cheapest ways to buy even if they seem the most convenient.

Let me give you an example. I recently fulfilled the promise I had made years ago to buy my wife a car. We found the perfect model, a three-year-old, sky blue Fiat 500 which had only 7,500 miles on the clock, and the proverbial 'one careful lady owner'. Perfect. The salesperson was very happy to offer me finance, as I didn't have the cash needed just sitting around. The monthly payments were certainly manageable, and he assured me that 6.9% interest was very reasonable, which it is if you compare it to the rates of 20% plus that credit card companies charge. However, after a few minutes' research, I discovered that my bank would lend me the same amount at 2.9% interest. If you have to borrow, make sure you are getting the best rate.

I know what I said earlier about borrowing for cars which depreciate, and the principle is a good one. In this case, however, the debt is manageable and the independence it will provide is worth the outlay. It is an example of the right purchase at the right price and with the lowest interest rate. I could have paid upfront instead of borrowing, but the money I had was invested and earning more than the 2.9% interest I paid.

What happens if you have already spent too much, you are behind with the repayments and threatening letters are starting to arrive - and you don't know what to do next? What not to do is to bury your head in the sand and hope it will go away, because it won't. The situation has to be faced and sorted. In most cases, you will discover that it is not as bad as you had feared. If you google debt advice or debt counselling, the first organisations which come up are those that will do the job for you but for a fee. You don't need to use them as there are a number of places to get help for free. Keep scrolling down and you will come to Christians Against Poverty and a number of other charities which specialise in this field, and who will help you get yourself sorted for free. Helpful organisations are listed in the Additional Resources at the end of the book.

Debt usually builds up when we are not aware of our spending and not considering our budget, but it is not always our own fault. My personal rule is that I must not buy something unless I know exactly how I am going to pay for it. If I need to use credit then I must know how much that credit costs and how I am going to pay it off. Credit card debt really does limit your freedom; as the Proverbs quote earlier in this chapter reminds us, 'the borrower is slave to the lender' (22:7).

Chapter 13
Storehouses

The answer to debt is in the storehouse. We read: 'The wise store up choice food and olive oil, but fools gulp theirs down'[94] and 'The Lord will command the blessing on you in your storehouses and in all to which you set your hand, and He will bless you in the land which the Lord your God is giving you.'[95] The way not to get into debt is by having enough money saved up before we buy. That's why we need a storehouse of money, so that we can use it when needed and not have to borrow. It's all very well to say that, but how can we save when there's nothing left at the end of the month to save with?

The answer is to put aside money when we have just been paid. Think about it: the vast majority of our money just comes in and goes out, towards rent or mortgages, car payments and utilities, mobile phone companies and supermarkets. Most of our money hardly stays long enough in our accounts to be called ours! You can decide to change that and keep more for yourself. Set up another account just for savings, to transfer cash into as soon as you are paid so that it is out of your current account. If it stays in your current account it will get spent. As I introduced in Chapter 11, those of you who are old enough may remember your mother or grandmother dividing up the cash each week as dad or grandad was paid. She probably had a number of jars or envelopes into which she divided the money: one jar for the rent, one for fuel, one for food shopping. Having a second or several bank accounts is just the jar principle brought up to date.

Pay God first, then pay yourself. Aim to live on no more than eighty per cent of your income, and pray! If you have given to God first, it's amazing how he will bless and enlarge what is left. If the thought of trying to live on eighty per cent of your income sounds impossible then start more slowly. Give five per cent to God and save five per cent, and see how you cope living on ninety per cent; then gradually increase both your giving and saving.

Ideally, after you have given your first ten per cent or more to the Lord, your next ten per cent is for saving and should be broadly divided into three jars, or storehouses. The first storehouse is for your short-term savings for emergency spending and holidays. This is vital at any age and should be built up before the others. The second storehouse is for the medium-term or mid-life expenses in life: money which you will need to spend in the next five to fifteen years. That could be on a new car, bigger house or children's educational costs. This one is less important if you are nearing retirement; most of those needs will have passed, and it's time to be fully concentrating on expanding your third storehouse - which is your retirement fund. Who is going to pay you when you are too old to work? The balance between these storehouses depends on your age and family situation. The need for medium-term savings will be much greater for a thirty-year-old with a young family than for someone nearing or at retirement.

Storehouses

1 2 3

Emergency Cash · Mid-Life Savings · Retirement Fund

Storehouse 1: emergency cash

It's important, first of all, to accumulate at least three months' worth (and preferably six months' worth) of net (after-tax) income in a bank account before you start on the other two storehouses. This money is there to take care of your short-term needs for cash. If the car breaks down, the boiler or washing machine needs replacing, or you find yourself between jobs then you have this cash reserve. Ideally, you should add to this figure the expected annual holiday spending money, too. If you need to spend some or all of it, make sure you rebuild that reserve as quickly as possible.

Without this emergency fund, what do we do? We reach for the credit card! Accumulating this cash reserve is your insurance against credit card debt. This money should be immediately accessible; a bank or building society deposit account will be fine. This should add at least a small amount of interest to your cash. Your emergency-cash storehouse will keep you out of debt.

Storehouse 2: mid-life savings

The second storehouse is for those chunky purchases that you may need to make in the medium term, in around the next five to fifteen years, such as new cars, children's educational/university expenses, and property upgrading or moving home. Items like these tend to be financed on borrowed money, but building a storehouse is a much better way. If you find that you don't need to use it all, then it becomes a good boost to your retirement savings. Think about it; if you borrow you have to repay with interest. That repayment money comes from current and ongoing income. If you are using your income to repay debt then it is not available for storehouse filling.

This money should be placed in investment or mutual funds. If you leave it in a bank or building society it will hardly grow. In fact, inflation (which just means that things become more expensive every year) will reduce the value of your cash, as the rate of inflation is almost always greater than the rate of interest added; something I will explain in Chapter 15.

Storehouse 3: retirement fund

The third storehouse is your retirement or pension fund. Here you may have some assistance from your employer, who may pay a percentage of your earnings into a pension scheme, usually on condition that you do the same. If your employer will match your contributions then it is wise to pay in up to the maximum that your company will match.

Someone once asked me whether pension saving was biblical as there is no reference to the idea of pensions in the Bible? Good question. The concept of retirement, the ability to withdraw from the labour market in later life, is largely a modern, western one. In ancient times, and in many parts of the world today, the idea of stopping work to enjoy oneself was unknown. The pattern of life was such that the older generation taught the younger, and continued to do less strenuous work and look after the grandchildren. This all made perfect sense when humans lived as subsistence farmers in extended family groups and villages. However, with the industrial revolution came the idea that it was reasonable to stop work at around age seventy, after a lifetime of toil in the factory.

The first private pension plan was introduced by the American Express Company in 1875. Germany was the first country to introduce a state pension scheme in 1889. Britain's state pension was launched in 1908, paying workers the princely sum of 5 shillings a week when they reached seventy years of age. This was not overgenerous when you consider the average life expectancy in those days was forty-seven years (although if a man reached seventy he was expected to live nearly another eight and a half years). In 1925, the scheme became contributory, which means that workers had to pay in while they were working in order to draw a pension at retirement. Nowadays, we expect to retire at around sixty-five and enjoy life for at least another twenty years.

Expecting to rely on the state pension in our old age is a recipe for poverty. The state pension, certainly in the UK, is one big Ponzi scheme! (Charles Ponzi was a swindler in the US in the 1920s, and gave his name to investment scams that promise high returns but in reality pay off the initial investors with the money raised from subsequent contributors.) This is because the contributions that today's workers pay into the state scheme immediately go out again to pay today's pensioners. There is no accumulating state pension fund. What this means is that the UK's state pension can only ever provide to its recipients amounts which can be extracted from today's workers without causing rebellion, uprising or civil disobedience. This is never going to be enough to give us the standard of living we would like to have. Currently, it pays twenty-nine per cent of average earnings.

Beware of complacency! In the last few years, auto-enrolment schemes have been introduced in the UK, where you contribute five per cent of your salary and your employer pays in three per cent. This is a good step forward but, even if you have a pension scheme with your employment, unless you are a very senior director you will only have around eight per cent of your income being invested, which will produce an income of around twenty-five per cent of your final salary.

If you are self-employed, these schemes do not include you; you need to take complete responsibility for your retirement funding. Ideally, you should be putting at least fifteen per cent of your income away each year in total for retirement. How many self-employed workers are investing at that level? And it is important not to put off starting to save, if you're self-employed. The length of time that an investment is held is almost as important as the amount invested. Start small and increase year by year.

In a 2018 survey of those over fifty by Aviva, it was found that only twenty-two per cent had started to take retirement saving seriously.[96] About forty-one per cent had no idea what they would need, or had started to calculate what they should save. Around twenty-four per cent of workers hoped an inheritance would fund their twilight years, and thirteen per cent were depending on a lottery win! How many of us have any idea what our current arrangements are liable to generate? We should check out exactly what our current schemes will provide. Don't let retirement be an unpleasant surprise. Rather than retirement becoming the time to stop work and put our feet up, I prefer to think of it as an opportunity to do something different with our time without having to be concerned about money.

It's true that the idea of pensions is not specifically there in the Bible, but there are clear references to the idea of gathering today for later use. At the beginning of this chapter I quoted Deuteronomy 28, about the Lord commanding a blessing on our storehouses. The very essence of a storehouse implies stockpiling today for using later. Joseph, for example, collected the produce of Egypt during the seven years of abundance and stored it in order to feed the surrounding nations in the seven years of famine which followed (Gen. 41:48-57). The Bible also gives us an example from nature: 'You lazy fool, look at an ant. Watch it closely; let it teach you a thing or two. Nobody has to tell it what to do. All summer it stores up food; at harvest it stockpiles provisions.'[97]

Our savings are our storehouses, and we need to fill them up. No one else will take responsibility for our future. And take heart from Deuteronomy 8 verse 18: 'Remember the Lord your God, for it is he who gives you the ability to produce wealth.'

Chapter 14
Family Money Management

Although every couple is different, the laws of economics do not change: the amount of money coming in needs to exceed the money being spent. One of the most common causes of divorce are financial problems. These are frequently triggered because people bring differing financial expectations and habits into a relationship. It's very important to communicate honestly and fully about our attitudes to money and how we have handled our finances in the past; ideally, before we pool all our resources. This way we can spot potential issues before they arise. It's important to discuss ambitions regarding what sort of lifestyle we want to lead: do we want the affluent, 'keeping up with the Joneses' style, or are we frugal by nature and more concerned with recycling everything? How are we going to deal with any debts that either party might bring into the marriage? Is one a spender and one a saver? What are our thoughts about having children; how many do we want and how do we want to provide for them?

Marriage is about two becoming one, and that union should include finances. If we embark on a marriage without clarity and openness about our financial situation, especially if we are in debt, then we are setting ourselves up for problems later. Love can overcome all sorts of issues but is severely tested by deception in the financial area.

It's a good idea to do your own credit check so you can see how the financial world views your handling of money. If either of you has a bad credit score then this can be a reason to keep your finances separate, at least for a time until it can be improved, since applying for a joint bank account or joint mortgage will be affected by the lower rating.

Broadly, there are two main ways to structure your everyday family finances: either share and manage everything as a couple in one joint bank account, or keep your separate accounts and both pay into a joint account to cover household bills. The advantage of the first method is that of simplicity; all income goes in and all spending and saving comes out of the one account. You can both see exactly where your money is going. This method is great if you are both in receipt of fixed salaries which have already had tax deducted. Agreement needs to be reached about how much each one can spend on personal items each month before having to seek the other's clearance. The second method can be helpful if one or both of you is self-employed and receiving an irregular income which also has to be declared for tax at a later date.

My wife and I operate a system which combines both methods. Our regular income is pooled and the household bills (including our giving and saving) are covered by it. Since I have some other self-employed, untaxed income, I keep this in a separate account, which makes it much easier to identify the amounts on which tax needs to be paid. All our accounts, including those for saving and giving, are visible to both of us. That there should be nothing hidden between us provides a basis for trust and security in our marriage.

Usually one will be more proficient at handling money than the other, and is therefore best placed to keep track of the budget. Both, however, should participate in budgetary discussions and decisions, however boring one of you may find this. Once a month, review your situation. Ask yourselves if the last month has gone to plan; have you underspent or overspent? Are there any adjustments that need to be made for the following month? At the beginning of each year, set yourselves agreed financial goals. Decide what you want to achieve in the coming year, which could be increasing your giving, or saving for a special holiday. If it is debt reduction, agree how much you want to pay off over the year and how you are going to do it. You are much more likely to achieve a goal to which you both are committed.

Most importantly, pray together about your money. Ask God to help you set your priorities and ask him to multiply your resources. He has a good track record of assistance when asked.

Teaching your children

Children learn primarily from what we do rather than what we say. They will absorb our financial priorities and values, and follow our actions not our words. According to a 2013 study by the University of Cambridge,[98] children's money habits are formed by the age of seven years. For this reason, integrity and scrupulous honesty in all our dealings is vital. If we try to 'get away with' anything deceitfully, we will undermine all that we would teach about honesty.

It's good to involve our children in the household shopping at an early age, comparing the costs of different items and involving them in the decision-making process. This is much more effective if you can pay cash, as you can have a finite amount with you. If your child wants something extra you can explain that you may not have enough for the other things they want to buy.

The lesson of having to wait to buy something you really want is a hard one to learn at any age. However, the sooner a child gains the ability to delay gratification, the better. This is much more important than it first appears, as a famous study in 1972 by researchers at Stanford University[99] demonstrated in the 'marshmallow experiment'. They put children into a room by themselves with a marshmallow on a table in front of them, and told them that if they could wait until the researcher returned before eating it then they would be given a second marshmallow; however, if they ate the first before his return, there would be no second. The children were filmed during the 15 minutes that the researcher was out of the room. Some children ate the marshmallow right away, some resisted for a time and then ate, and a few held out to receive the second marshmallow. This experiment was repeated by other researchers[100] who then tracked the children over several years. The ones who had been able to resist until the second marshmallow appeared were shown to be more successful, fitter and happier than the others.

When children start receiving an allowance, find three jars and label them 'giving', 'saving' and 'spending'. Agree with them how much they are going to put into each jar. The earlier the giving and savings habits become part of their lives the better. Allow them to earn more through household chores to show them that work has a value and money needs to be earned. Once they are old enough to understand, have them join in your monthly budget reviews.

Peer pressure brings on the 'must have' syndrome. Challenging to counter, one strategy is to get out all of your child's 'must have' items bought over the last few years and ask them why they wanted it, and how often they have used or worn it. Teach them to pray for the things they want.

Brands and designer labels are a real pain. I remember buying my eldest his first pair of soccer boots. On the basis that he would grow out of them within a few months, I wanted to buy a well-known but cheap pair. His reaction was one of horror, 'I can't go to school with those, people will laugh at me!' Needless to say, I did succumb and bought a much more expensive pair. Looking back, I clearly wasted an opportunity for a meaningful discussion about values and peer pressure. It's even more difficult today. A smartphone seems to be indispensable equipment for everyone as soon as they can talk. Yet if we don't teach our children how to handle money, we leave them at the mercy of the advertisers and marketers.

Here are some simple tips for raising responsible children:

1 Start them saving early, not with a piggy bank but using a transparent jar so they can see the money building up.

2 When they want to purchase toys they see at the shops, have them take the cash out of their jars so they can make the connection and see that when it's gone, it's gone.

3 As they grow, help them make good decisions by learning that they have choices over how they spend their cash.

4 Don't take them to toy shops unless you intend to buy toys. This may seem obvious but, depending on the age of your child, the idea of window shopping for some future purchase just doesn't work.

5 Allow them to earn by doing extra household chores; this builds the connection between work and money.

6 As they grow, help them to become more independent, letting them choose their own clothes, toiletries and other personal items within a fixed budget.

Successful money management for couples and families relies on clear and open communication. If big decisions need to be made then each family member should be involved once they are old enough to understand. Either you will shape your family's finances or the advertisers will. The choice is yours.

Chapter 15
Investment for Beginners

Is it important to learn something about investment? This is where eyes start to glaze over and some people switch off completely. Please don't! My intention is not to turn you into a financial adviser, but to give you enough information to be able to talk sensibly to one. You really don't have to learn anything about investment if you are content just to receive a meagre return from your bank deposit account and trust your employer to have chosen the right funds for your pension scheme. If you are in a pension scheme then you are already an investor. Apart from purchasing your house, you will be putting more money into your pension scheme than anything else in your life. Almost your largest lifetime purchase! You are already investing, so it is worth trying to understand a bit about it.

Investment can seem quite complicated. Simply, investment can be defined as the act of putting money towards an endeavour with the expectation of obtaining additional income or profit. Warren Buffett, one of the world's best known and most successful investors, describes investing as 'the process of laying out money now to receive more in the future'. The purpose of investing is to put your money to work in one or more types of investment vehicle, in the hope of growing that money over time. In other words, making your money work for you rather than you work for your money.

Assets

There a number of different ways to go about it, but investing boils down to choosing which type of asset suits you best. At its most basic, there are four main classes of asset you can invest in.

Cash

Just about everybody is familiar with cash as an investment. You place it in a bank or building society, and they pay you some interest on your money for as long as you have it there. There are different types of accounts according to how long you want to leave your money; some with fixed rates of interest, some variable. Basically, the longer you agree to leave it with them, the more interest they will pay you. Interest rates change according to the economic climate, and the rate of interest on your money can go up or down. Some banks will offer a fixed rate for a certain length of time, typically one, two, three and five years. Interest rates are low, post COVID-19 pandemic, to stimulate growth in the economy.

Bonds or fixed income funds

Bonds or fixed income funds are products to allow governments and companies to borrow money over a specific period of time. The product which the government issues is known as gilt-edged stocks, or gilts for short, so named because the certificate has a gilt-colour edge. They guarantee a fixed level of interest over the period and your money back at the end. Lending to government is seen as virtually risk free; and it is, provided you can hold your investment to maturity. The yield (interest rate) is higher than that from cash on deposit in the bank.

Shares

Shares are issued by companies that wish to raise money for expansion. Owning shares means that you own a small portion of the company concerned, and each year are entitled to a small part of the profit made. If the company does well then you will do well; conversely, if the company does badly then so will you. If you buy the right shares, you make serious money - and likewise, the converse is also true.

Property

Property is something that most of us understand. We have a belief that house prices always keep rising (untrue) and recognise that property let to tenants generates income (hopefully). Property can work very well as an investment, but it can also be a nightmare. Bad tenants, maintenance costs and mortgage rates can easily mess up your cash flow.

Income derived from asset classes

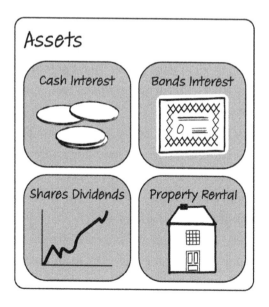

With the exception of more exotic investments such as commodities (gold, precious metals, art, classic cars, etc.) all others are a variation on one of these four types. While every investment vehicle has its positives and negatives, the most important investment is always in God's kingdom and should be made first. This is the only investment you can make where you can't lose.

Where should your money be saved?

For your emergency fund (storehouse 1), a deposit account with a bank or building society is the right place for your money. This is instantly accessible and produces a small amount of interest. However, over the longer term (storehouses 2 or 3) it is not such a good place. The problem is that although your money is safe in the bank, it will gradually decline in real value over time because of inflation. The rate of interest that you can earn from the bank will always be lower than the rate of inflation (with the possible exception of some short-term special deals).

Your longer-term savings will gain far more in investment funds. The value will fluctuate over the short term but can be expected to give superior returns over the medium to longer term, but fear of loss can cause you to put all of your money into bank or building society deposit accounts. That fear usually originates from not understanding how investment works.

Deciding which shares or bonds you wish to hold can take a lot of time and energy. Most of us do not have large amounts of money to invest so we cannot afford to buy many different companies' shares. Choosing the right shares is the key to success or failure in investing. The level of risk if you have shares in only two or three different companies is very high; if one of those companies goes bust, it's a big chunk of your money gone. Since most of us have neither the time nor the inclination to research company details and read the annual reports, I have always recommended investment funds for the beginner.

An investment fund can be simply described as a large bucket into which lots of people put their money. This means that many different company shares can be purchased and the risk is dramatically reduced. But the right ones still have to be chosen, so someone who knows what they are doing (such as an investment manager) invests the cash across a large number of companies on your behalf. In this way, you spread your investment over a lot of different shares and bonds. This is known as 'diversification' and reduces risk.

If your investment manager is good then you will do well. They will buy and sell the shares according to their judgement regarding the prospects for that company. This is called 'active' management. The manager takes a fee, usually as a percentage of your fund each year, as their reward. There is an alternative method of investment management known as 'passive' investment. This where a fund manager buys all the shares in a particular index, such as the FTSE 100 which is an index of the 100 largest companies quoted on the UK stock market, and your return will mirror the growth of those companies. This method is cheaper than the active method as it requires much less management. Personally, I like to spread my investments between the two types.

Let's talk about risk

Risk brings to mind winning or losing, gambling or speculating; the National Lottery or betting on a horse race. When the investment industry talks about risk, it means the degree to which the value of a particular investment will potentially rise or fall over the next year, despite black Mondays and financial crises.

The extreme reaction to the COVID-19 pandemic has meant global stock markets falling by around thirty per cent of their value. Individuals would have only lost thirty per cent if they had sold their investments at that time. As I write, a few weeks into the lockdown, markets have already recovered about a third of the losses. Holding on, I believe, will see values bounce back over the next twelve months as life returns to normal. Thus, now is the time to buy rather than sell. Many people make the mistake of buying when things are going well and market values are high, and then selling when markets have dropped. That is the way to lose money. One of the best ways to mitigate investment risk is by regular monthly contributions which will help smooth out the ups and downs of the market. It is impossible to invest anywhere without some degree of risk.

While your money is safe in a bank and is even protected against the bank going bust (in the UK, up to £85,000), inflation will steadily erode the value of that money as the annual rate of inflation is around 2%. An investment fund is much more likely to beat inflation, usually by a good margin, but the capital is not guaranteed, and the value will fluctuate. As long as you are investing for five years or longer, the returns from an investment fund should handsomely beat a deposit. However, there will be good years and not so good years for investment returns within that time. You should expect an average annual return of five to six per cent[101] after charges in a fund; that is the average for the last twenty-five years in the UK. Your interest from cash in the bank is one to one and a half per cent, at best.

You may feel that you would rather put your money into bricks and mortar, as the beauty of property is such that you can see and touch it. Property can be a very good investment, but it is not without its own risks. Let's say you opted for the most popular form of property investment, which is buying another house or flat to let. You usually have to borrow money to buy property, which means that if you don't have a tenant paying rent then it's costing you money not only to service that loan, but also to pay the council tax on the property.

Property needs maintenance. If you buy a flat then you will pay a service charge to a management company to cover maintenance. If you buy a house then it will generate the usual bills for things going wrong and wearing out. And property is not liquid. That may seem to be stating the obvious, but what I mean is that your investment cannot be bought and sold quickly, nor can you sell a part of a property if you need some cash.

Do you really want to become a landlord? Tenants can be unpredictable and sometimes not just awkward but dishonest. I spoke to one investor with many properties who said that approximately one out of every twelve tenancies he arranged went wrong! Having said all that, property has still been the asset in the UK that has grown the fastest over the last twenty-five years, with house prices at least three times higher over that period.[102]

Although there is much more to know if you are going to choose your own investments and monitor them; however, that's all you need to know if you are going to find a good financial adviser and take their advice. Every authorised financial adviser has to be qualified to a high level and will be listed on the Financial Conduct Authority's register. The best way to find a good financial advisor is by personal recommendation from others who have used them. Do not take investment advice from the person in the pub or anyone who is poorer than you are. If anybody is recommending particular shares to you, ask them how much they have invested in that particular company! Stay well away from bitcoin and other cryptocurrencies; the swings in their values really do make this gambling, not investing. Likewise with day trading, contracts for difference and foreign exchange trading. Give them all a wide berth. Never invest with someone who telephones or cold calls you offering shares. These are always scams, as cold calling to sell investments is illegal in the UK. In short, don't be afraid of investment, but do use an expert.

In Matthew 25, the parable of the talents makes it clear that Jesus expects us to use money to make money, i.e. investment, at the very least to put it in the bank rather than under the mattress. In other words, good stewardship is about investing wisely rather than just preservation.

Reflect on your own attitudes to investment. Are they conditioned by faith or fear?

Chapter 16
Eight Keys to Abundant Living

An abundant life is more than just having enough money. It's living in the good of God's blessing. An abundant life is enjoying the love lavished on us by our heavenly Father and living life with confidence that God is on our side, that we need have no fear of the future as we know he will take care of us. A financially abundant life is not necessarily a sign of spiritual maturity, but a combination of the favour of the Lord and our recognition that his favour is upon us. Jesus said, 'I have come that they may have life, and that they may have *it* more abundantly' (John 10:10, NKJV).

If you find that you are worrying about money, then you have not yet stepped into the abundant life. The abundant life means that you have enough money not to feel you lack anything you need, and you have complete trust in God to provide for the future.

Let me summarise the eight key steps:

1 Believe that God wants to bless you. Thank him daily for his provision.

2 Speak positively about your financial situation, both current and future.

3 Consciously be seeking the kingdom first.

4 Be generous, give to God consistently and pray.

5 Ensure that all your financial dealings are righteous.

6 Get out of debt as soon as possible.

7 Budget to ensure wise spending.

8 Build your storehouses.

Moses describes God's heart for our wellbeing perfectly, in Deuteronomy 30. Picture the scene: Moses is about to die, and the Israelites are about to enter the Promised Land. He has been reminding them of the terms of the covenant, and the blessings and curses which would come upon them according to their behaviour. Apart from a final word of blessing over each of the tribes, these are his last words:

When all these blessings and curses I have set before you come on you and you take them to heart wherever the Lord your God disperses you among the nations, and when you and your children return to the Lord your God and obey him with all your heart and with all your soul according to everything I command you today, then the Lord your God will restore your fortunes and have compassion on you and gather you again from all the nations where he scattered you. Even if you have been banished to the most distant land under the heavens, from there the Lord your God will gather you and bring you back. He will bring you to the land that belonged to your ancestors, and you will take possession of it. He will make you more prosperous and numerous than your ancestors. The Lord your God will circumcise your hearts and the hearts of your descendants, so that you may love him with all your heart and with all your soul, and live. The

Lord your God will put all these curses on your enemies who hate and persecute you. You will again obey the Lord and follow all his commands I am giving you today. Then the Lord your God will make you most prosperous in all the work of your hands and in the fruit of your womb, the young of your livestock and the crops of your land. The Lord will again delight in you and make you prosperous, just as he delighted in your ancestors, if you obey the Lord your God and keep his commands and decrees that are written in this Book of the Law and turn to the Lord your God with all your heart and with all your soul. (Deuteronomy 30:1-10)

Thank you for walking through this journey with me. I trust it has been helpful and that you are looking expectantly to a more positive financial future. As you go on to put it all into practice, I wish you every blessing, not only financially but, most of all, that your relationship with God will deepen as you realise just how good he really is. Or, as Jesus put it in the Sermon on the Mount (Matt. 6:33): 'But seek first his kingdom and his righteousness, and all these things will be given to you as well'.

Additional Resources

Moving from negative to positive mindsets

Dr Caroline Leaf: https://drleaf.com
Steve Backlund, Igniting Hope Ministries: https://ignitinghope.com

Debt reduction and money management

UK government Money Advice Service:
https://www.moneyadviceservice.org.uk
Citizens Advice UK: https://www.citizensadvice.org.uk
Christians Against Poverty: https://capuk.org
Dave Ramsey: https://daveramsey.com

Economic living

https://www.moneysavingexpert.com
Consumers' Association: https://www.which.co.uk/money/money-saving-tips

Evidence for God at work

Farming God's Way: https://www.farming-gods-way.org
The Simon Abundance Index, updated 2019: https://www.cato.org/blog/simon-abundance-index-r-2019
Renewal Journal: https://renewaljournal.com

Acknowledgements

First, thank you, Father God, whose Spirit inspired and enabled me from start to finish.

Then my thanks to Burt and Barb Horowitz for taking Anne and me to that small prayer meeting in Gary, Indiana, where Sandra prophesied this book. Without that I would probably never have started.

To those others who have encouraged me along the way or let me use their stories or have given me valuable feedback, particularly Julian and Katia Adams, Jules Jonker, Wendy Mann, Nick Gore, Matt Tipper, Phil Cox, Tony Coggan, Chris Bullivant, Andy Hawkins, Roydon Loveley, Chris Vincent, Sarah Amies, Tim Davies, Dom Llewellyn, Dan, Ben and Tim. Please forgive me if I have forgotten anyone.

Thanks to Ali Green, my editor, who turned my writing into readable English, and to Liz Barras for her visuals and cover idea.

To my darling, long-suffering wife, Anne, who has put up with my obsession to complete this book instead of retiring gracefully, thank you.

Endnotes

Introduction
2. Gerten, Dieter, Heck, Vera, et al. (2020) Feeding ten billion people is possible within four terrestrial planetary boundaries. *Nature Sustainability* 3, 200-208.
3. Hill, Craig, Five Wealth Secrets (Family Foundations International 2012)
4. Kiyosaki, Robert T, Rich Dad Poor Dad (Paradise Valley AZ. TechPress Inc 1997)

Chapter 1
5. 2 Chr. 26:5
6. Gen. 2:12
7. Gen. 14:4
8. Gen. 26:13
9. Gen. 28:22
10. Deut. 8:18

Chapter 2
11. Matt. 2:14
12. 2 Cor. 8:9
13. Luke 4:18,19
14. John 2:1-10
15. Mark 6:37
16. Mark 8:1-10
17. Matt. 6,7
18. Luke 18:18-30
19. Luke 8:3
20. Matt. 25:14-30
21. Rom. 9-11
22. 3 John 2 HCSB

Chapter 3
23. Matt. 19:21
24. 2 Cor. 8:9
25. Rom. 5:1
26. 1Tim. 6:10
27. Miller, David W. 'Wealth Creation as Integrated with Faith: A Protestant Reflection'. 23 April 2007. Conference address, Notre Dame, IN, USA: Hesburgh Center.

28. Mark 10:17-31

29.Willard D. (1988) *The Spirit of the Disciplines: Understanding How God Changes Lives* (San Francisco: Harper and Rowe

Chapter 4

30. Meadows, Donella H., Meadows, Dennis L., Randers Jorgen & Behrens III, William Wk. (1972) The Club of Rome. *The Limits to Growth.* (Falls Church, VA, USA: Potomac Associates).

31.Ehrlich, Paul R.& Ehrlich, Anne (1968) *The Population Bomb.* (New York City: Sierra Club/Ballantine Books).

32. Simon, Julian L. (1981) *The Ultimate Resource.* (Princeton, NJ, USA: Princeton University Press).

33. Pooley, Gale I. & Tupy, Marian L. (2018) 'The Simon Abundance Index: A New Way to Measure Availability of Resources.' Paper. Washington, DC: Cato Institute, 4 Dec.

34.Sanyal, Sanjeev (2013) 'Predictions of a Rogue Demographer.' Frankfurt: Deutsche Bank (cited in the *Telegraph*, 6 August 2019, by Daniel Hannan).

35. Eph. 2:6

36. Ps. 50:10

37. Matt. 10:38

38. Rom. 6:11

Chapter 5

39. Matt. 26:11

40. Deut. 24:21

41. Mark 10:21

42 Luke 8:3

43. Matt. 25:14-30

44. Otis, George Jr (2014) 'Twenty-first Century Revivals: Transforming Revivals.' *Renewal Journal*, 28 April: www.renewaljournal.com

45. Matt. 6:33

Chapter 6

46. Prov. 23:7, NKJV

47. Phil. 4:8

48. 1 Tim. 5:17

49. Matt. 12:34b, NKJV

50. Eph. 6:12

51. Ps. 39:14

52. Rev. 1:6, NKJV

53. Phil. 14:19

54. 2 Cor. 9:10,11a

55. Luke 10:27

Chapter 7

56. Gen. 4:4

57. 2 Cor. 9:6

58. Luke. 6:38

59. Deut. 14:23

60. Deut. 26:12

61. Exod. 35:5

62. Luke 11:42; Matt. 23:23

63. Acts 15:28,29

64. 1 Tim. 5:17,18

65. 1 Cor. 9:11

66. Prov. 3:9; 11:24

67. Mal. 3:8-10

68. 2 Cor. 9:7

69. Exod. 25:2

70. Whillans, A.V, Dunn, E.W., Sandstrom, G.M., Dickerson, S.S. & Madden, K.M. (2016) Is spending money on others good for your heart? *Health Psychology* 35(6), 574-583.

71. Konrath, Sara & Brown, Stephanie (2011) 'The Effects of Giving on Givers.' In Roberts, N. & Newman, M. eds, *Handbook of Health and Social Relationships* (Washington, DC: APA Books).

72. Dunn, E.W., Aknin, L.B. & Norton, M.I. (2008) Spending money on others promotes happiness. *Science* 319, 1687-1688.

73. Dulleck, U., Shaffner, M. & Torgler, B. (2014) Heartbeat and Economic Decisions. Observing Mental Stress Among Proposers and Responders in the Ultimatum Bargaining Game. *PLOS ONE*, 23 Sept: https://doi.org/10.1371/journal.pone.0108218

74. Poulin, M.J., Brown, S.L., Dillard, A.J. & Smith, D.M. (2013) *American Journal of Public Health* 103(9), 1649-1655.

75. *State of our Unions.* (2011) Report. National Marriage Project. (Charlottesville: University of Virginia). Quoted by Smalley, Greg (2020) in 'Generosity in Marriage: Small Acts That Make a Big Difference'. Focus on the Family, 16 Jan.

Chapter 8
76. Josh. 1:8
77. Luke 5:1-11
78. 1 Tim. 6:10
79. Matt. 6:33

Chapter 9
80. Titus 3:1
81. Lev. 19:11, NKJV
82. Ezek. 28:1-19
83.John 10:10
84. Ps. 18:20
85. Prn ov. 21:21
86. 1 Tim.5:8

Chapter 11
87. Prov.21:20, NLT
88. Deut.8:18
89. Matt. 5:42

Chapter 12
90. Eph. 5:16
91. Matt. 5:42
92. TUC. News listing. www.tuc.org.uk/news/unsecured-debt-hits-new-peak-£15400-household---new-tuc-analysis [accessed 13 April 2020].
93. Money Advice Service (2018) Press release, 12 Nov.''£96 billion of debt hidden from friends and family.' London: Money Advice Service.

Chapter 13
94. Prov. 21:20
95. Deut. 28:8, NKJV
96. Aviva Pensions Report (2018) 'Retirement Reality.' 28 Nov.
97. Prov. 6:6-8, MSG

Chapter 14
98. Whitebread, D. & Bingham, S. (2013) *Habit Formation and Learning in Young Children.* Cambridge: University of Cambridge/London: Money Advisory Service, May.

99. Mischel, Ebbeson, & Zeiss (1972) 'Cognitive and Attentional Mechanisms in Delay of Gratification.' *Journal of Personality and Social Psychology* 21(2), 204-218.
100. Stephanie M. Carlson and University of Washington, Seattle (2012)

Chapter 15.
101. 'What are the average returns of the FTSE 100?' www.ig.com [accessed 30 April 2020].
102. Halifax UK Property Index. www.halifax.co.uk